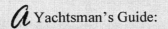

𝒶 Yachtsman's Guide:

Smuggling Your Boat Out of Jail

*The Foreign & State-to-State Maze
of Cruising Regulations:
Avoiding the Snares & Traps*

D1104320

by

Captain Michael P. Maurice

of the

United States Merchant Marine

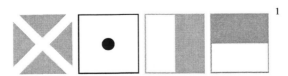[1]

---

[1] MIKE

Copyright © 2007 by Michael P. Maurice

Maurice, Michael P., 1946 –

Softcover Perfect Binding ISBN: 978-0-9831757-0-4
Softcover Coil Binding ISBN: not assigned
Hardcover Dust Jacket ISBN: not assigned
Hardcover Casewrap ISBN: not assigned

First Edition

Dedication

My parents: Gordon and Dorothy, who taught me to read and write. My
wife Pamela: who helps me assemble the Cadillac smuggled out *One Piece
at a Time,* and Johnny Cash: who taught us all how to do it.

To order copies: contact the author

http://tinyurl.com/39lac6 [i]

 +1-503-694-5267, or 624-5895

Credits

Photos

Front Cover: NOAA Chart, Pacific Ocean, 1941

■ - "L" - Stop Immediately

⊠ - "V" - I Require Assistance

Back Cover: Hakodate, Japan 2006

Page i: 52' Motor Lifeboat "Victory", U.S. Coast Guard Photo

Page ii: Dredge "Essayons", U.S. Army Corps of Engineers

Page xii: Japan 2006

Page xiv: Zhuhai, China 2006

By the Author, unless noted

Special Type Fonts

Manfred Klein

Cover Designs by Author

Roman Galleys: Ahoy!

Printed in the  United States of America

 Print Date 11/19/2010 12:02 PM

Table of Contents

Credits iii
    Photos iii
    Special Type Fonts iii

Forward .... *xiv*

Preface .... *xv*

Introduction .... *xvii*

Non-U.S. Boats & Citizens .... **xvii**

Corrections .... **xix**

Accuracy .... **xix**
    Report Errors xix

Label Making .... **xx**

Added for Completeness .... **xx**

Acknowledgements .... **xxi**
    Technical Advice xxi

Section 1 – ▷ Navigation Rules *1*

The Captain's Authority **1**

Unique COLREGS **2**

Variability in Laws, Regulations & Enforcement **3**

A History of Clearance Law **4**

Section 2 – ▶ Clearing *5*

Clearing In & Out of Foreign Countries **5**
    Night Entry or Leaving.. 5
    General 5
    U.S. Customs – Notice to Masters.. 7
    U.S. Customs Web Page for Travel-by-Boat Issues............ 7
    U.S. Know Before-You-Go Web Pages 7
        Visa Waiver Program 7
    Foreign Yachts Visiting the U.S.. 8
    Health 8
    Immigration 8
    Customs... 8
    Agriculture.. 8
    Clearing In 8

Clearing Out 8
Liquor 9
Rarely Asked for Documents 9
Dinghy-Tenders 9
Garbage – Refuse 9
Pumping Holding Tanks 10

Secured & Sealed in a Locker 10

Cruising License-Permits 10
United States 10
Successive Cruising Permits 12
U.S. Reciprocal Cruising License Countries 12
    Countries by Map Area 13
    A Horror Story 13
Other Countries 13
Length of Cruising Permits 13
    Countries with Liberal Permit Lengths 14
    Countries with Restrictive Permit Lengths 14

Exemption to a Formal Entry 14

Entering Without the Owner 15

Entering a Foreign Built Boat 15
Vessel Never Before Entered 15

Over 20 meters in Length 15

Yachts Over 100 Gross Tons 16

Commercial Versus, Recreational 16

Notice of Arrival 16
24?? Hour Warning 16
Where to Find Notice Times 17
Australia – AU 17

Finding Web Sites 18
Customs 18
General Searches on Google 19
Cruisers Information 19
Big Luxury Yachts 19

Crew Issues 19
    Crew Arriving to Join the Boat 20

Radio Licenses 21
Amateur (HAM) Radio 21
    Foreign Country Operation 21

IARP Countries 21
CEPT Countries..21

CB Radios...**21**

Handheld VHF Radios...**22**

Guns..**23**
Mexico...23
U.S. 23

Section 3 – ▶*Clearing Out*...*25*

A Real Short... Story **25**

Staying out of Jail...**25**

Checklist for Leaving the U.S........................................**25**
Title or Document 25
Clearance to Foreign Port...26
Fly the Flag of Your Country 26
Extra Copies 26
Ship's Stamp..27
Local Currency 27
Power of Attorney 27
Credit Cards..27
Picking Up/Buying a Yacht in a Foreign Country 27

Export Controlled Products **28**

Section 4 – ➤ *Offshore*..*30*

Ship's Identification **30**

Accident Offshore, Collision, Etc..................................**30**

Being Approached at Night **31**

Safety Boarding by Coast Guard **31**

Near Shore Cruising Obstacles **33**

Emergency Help **34**
U.S. Coast Guard Search & Rescue Centers 34
U.S. Embassy or State Department 34
Piracy...35
IMB Piracy Reporting Centre..35
U.S. Citizens While in Foreign Countries 35
Search & Rescue Insurance 36

Registering Beacons **36**
EPIRB – 406 MHz 36

Australia – AMSA.. 36
Other SAR Centers.. 37
UK Beacon Registration 37
EPIRB – 121.5 MHz 37

High Seas Law 37
Approached by Another Vessel... 37
Tactics for Right of Innocent Passage............................... 38
If Forced to Anchor... 39

Section 5 – ▷ Travel Documents *41*

Passport Renewals... 41

Travel Visas 41
For U.S. Citizens 42
For NON-U.S. Citizens 42
Visa Waiver Program (VWP) 42

Electronic Travel Authority ETA...................................... 43

Carnet... 43

Parts & Materials for a Vessel In-Transit 43

Section 6 – ▷ *45*

State-to-State.. *45*

Cruising Reciprocity Issues 45
Live Aboard 46
State Tax & Registration Issues 46
U.S. Documentation Issues 49

Section 7 – ▷ Pilotage *50*

U.S. Pilotage Requirements for Foreign Flag Yachts 50
Washington State Pilotage Waters 51
Pilotage & British Flagged Vessels..................................... 52
Foreign Flag Yachts & Pilotage 53
A History of Pilotage 54
Acting as Pilot... 54
Compulsory Pilotage, Foreign Yachts - U.S. West Coast.................. 54

Section 8 – ▷ *56*

U.S. Laws.. *56*

Ship's Station Licenses & Operator Permits........................ 56
Voluntary & Bridge-to-Bridge (B2B) Yachts................... 56
Installations 58

Bridge-to-Bridge Regulations (B2B) 58
    Subpart U, (80.1001–1023). 58
Great Lakes.. 58
Summary 58

Online Updating: FCC & EPIRB Information.................................**59**

U.S. Laws of Interest to Recreational Yachtsmen **60**
Summary of U.S. CFR 60
    Title 19 U.S. Customs: Parts 4, 148, 161, 162, 171 60
    Title 33 Navigation; Parts 26, 67, 80, 107, 110, 158–162, 164–
    167, 173–187, 207, 334.. 60
    Title 40 Environment: Parts 91, 94 61
    Title 46 Shipping: Parts 7, 24, 25, 67, 69, 159–164................... 61
    Title 47 Radio: Parts 80 (Subpart X), 97 62
    Title 50 Wildlife: Part 227.. 62
Cuba 62
U.S. Customs Regulations... 62
Notes for Non-U.S. Flag Vessels 63
U.S. Coast Pilots... 63

Section 9 – Medical *64*

Malaria & Yellow Fever **64**
Malaria Atlas Project.. 65

US Centers for Disease Control (CDC) **66**

Beef, Poultry, Meats, Vegetables & Fruits **66**

Night Vision..**67**
Web Site Resources.. 67

Section 10 – Navigation.. *68*

Buoy Systems A & B **68**

IALA Boundaries **69**
Maps.. 69
    Atlantic... 69
    Pacific... 69

Cardinal Marks **70**

Sailing Directions.. **71**
Vessel Traffic Services – VTS 71

Section 11 – Formal Ship's Business................................. *75*

Section 12 – Miscellaneous *76*

Single-Handing **76**
   AIS 76
   Lookout 76

Numbering & Documentation................................. **76**
   Vessel Tender Documented?.................................... 77
   Boat Name.. 78
   Numbered Vessels.. 78
   Documented Vessels 78
   Documentation, State Registration & Insurance 79

Earthquakes... **81**

Tsunami.. **81**

Grounding... **82**

Appendix.. *83*

☎International Telephone Dialing............................ **83**

U.S. Documentation Renewal................................. **86**

Cruising License Reciprocity **88**
   Title 19 CFR Section 4.94..................................... 88

Federally Licensed Pilot **88**

Internet Resources **89**
   FCC Ship's License Help... 89
   List of Customs Web Sites...................................... 89
     By Country 89
   Foreign Country's Embassies in US.......................... 89
   Embassies by Country... 89
   ⚑ ICC Commercial Commerce Piracy Page............. 90
   U.S. Internet Sources... 90
     United States International Trade Commission............ 90
     Flags 90
     Embassies, Consuls... 90
     State Department Notes, by Country....................... 90
     Pleasure Boats 90
   ⚑ Reporting Suspicious Activity 90
     U.S. Customs.. 90
     Customs Districts 90
   Establishing Residency 91
   U.S. Inland Cruising... 91
     Great Loop 91
     New York Canals 91
   European Cruising.. 91

Canal Regulations.. 91
Size information 91
RYA European Waterways Regulations 91
Foreign Cruising.. 91
International Certificate of Competency 91
Seasickness 91
Smuggling In the Old Days 91
Web Pages of Country Info 92
USCG Regulations 92
Light Lists 92
USCG 92
Notices to Mariners 92
Wiki – Notice to Mariners... 93
NGA Publications.. 93
Official Logbook, PDF 93
Articles of Agreement 93
U.S. Code Documents (USC)... 93
Current General Country Information 93
Shanghaiing 93
No Discharge Zones 93

Power of Attorney **94**
A Limited Durable Power of Attorney 94

Technical Contacts **95**
FLIR 95

Definitions **95**
Admiralty Law 95
Captain of Record.. 95
Clearance Form 95
COLREG 96
Law of the Sea (LOTS) 96
Other Definitions.. 98
AIS 98
Apostille 98
Carnet 98
Certified Copy 98
CFR 99
DSC – Digital Selective Calling... 99
EEZ – Exclusive Economic Zone... 99
NLR 99
Flag Country.. 99
Foreign Built Vessel 99
ITU 100

MMSI Number 100
Mutiny 100
No Cure, No Pay 100
Proof of Duty 100
Sail Vessel 101
State of Principle Use 101
U.S. Code of Federal Regulations (CFR) 101
USC 102
VAT – Value Added Tax 102
Voyage Data Recorder 102
Zarpe 102

Boating Regulations by U.S. STATE **102**

USCG National Vessel Documentation Center **102**
VDOC FAQ 103
Ordering Copies 103

Merchant Marine Officers Handbook **104**

World Wide **105**
Cruising Information 105
Embassy Web Sites 105

Table of Night Vision Properties **109**

U.S. State Tax Issues **110**
Definition of Real Versus Personal Property 110
Property Taxes 110
Picking A State 112
Definitions for State Table 113
    Consecutive 113
    Registration w/Validation Decal 113
Reciprocity at State Boundaries 113
Table of State Abbreviations & Boating Tax Administrators 114
Table of Boating Law Administrators 119
Alternate Numbers 119

State by State **122**
Registration Offices 122
    Phone Numbers, Reciprocity, Decals 122
Table of State Sales & Property Taxes for Boats 124
Table of State Fuel Taxes for Boats & Refunds 125
Coastal States w/Property Tax 128
    Property Tax States 128
Property Tax Exemption 128
Highest Sales Tax 129
Property & Sales Tax 131

Maps of Coastal U.S. Customs Districts **134**
    U.S. West Coast 134
    Canada – North Carolina 135
    North Carolina – Florida 136
    Brownsville, TX – Georgia 137
    Summary of U.S. Customs Districts & Ports 138
    Detail Table of U.S. Customs Districts & Ports 138

Innocent Passage – UN Law of the Sea **148**
    Part II TERRITORIAL SEA AND CONTIGUOUS ZONE 148

Territorial, Contiguous & EEZ Claims **153**

Duty Free Ports **157**

Capt. Mike's – General Standing Orders **161**

Bibliography *164*

General **164**

Recommended Reading List **164**
    The Language of Sailors 164

Smuggling in the Old Days **166**

INDEX *167*

Forthcoming Books from Capt. Mike *172*

Salvage - ✕ *172*
    BoatUS Salvage 172

End Notes *174*

Table of Figures

Figure 1 – Bill & Stella Kimley. Hard at Work, Building Diesel Ducks at Zhuhai, China. "So that others may live." xiv
Figure 2 – COLREGs & Inland Rules _____ xviii
Figure 3 – Japanese Navy Ship, Hakodate Harbor, Hokkaido Island, Japan _____ xxi
Figure 4 – Curious Japanese Fishermen Meet Americans __ 5
Figure 5 – U.S. Customs Web Page_____ 7
Figure 6 – Sample Cruising License _____ 11
Figure 7 – Sunset on Japanese Fishing Boat, Kushiro City Dock, Hokkaido Island _____ 24
Figure 8 - Japanese Bamboo Raft "Float" _____ 33
Figure 9 - Map of local hazards, Hakodate Japan _____ 34
Figure 10 – IALA Region Map _____ 69
Figure 11 – Cardinal Marks _____ 70
Figure 12 - Traffic Lanes, Strait of Juan De Fuca & BC __ 72
Figure 13 – Chart 18480-2, Quileute River, WA. Entrance 73
Figure 14 – Washington – California _____ 134
Figure 15 – Maine – North Carolina_____ 135
Figure 16 – North Carolina – Florida_____ 136
Figure 17 – Gulf Coast States _____ 137

You tie your boat up with a knot. Now if you went back in time, a thousand years or so, you might believe that *Your God* binds you to him with an *invisible* one. In which case, maybe you could bind him to you!

You take a piece of line and lay it on the ground. By itself, the line is nothing. But, make a knot and it binds him; to something, or some-one...

A kind of symbolic gesture—that reeks of magic! Of course, to the ignorant and supersti-tious mind of long ago...

Knots W E R E magic!

Welcome to the World of Sailors

Forward

 PEOPLE who boat, be it inland waters or offshore, share an Adventurous Spirit and value the freedom that is at the essence of being on the water. The goal of voyaging is to maximize boating pleasure and minimize boating hassles.

What Captain Mike has thoughtfully assembled is nothing less than a collection of precious gems. They are precious in that they have the ability to save our time, our money, preserve relationships, and inform us of some very nasty and obscure marine regulations.

Even if we are experienced yachtsmen, this compendium will serve to validate our understanding, or may provoke some further investigation. No other marine resource covers the range of topics, from naming your tender, being boarded by the Coast Guard, and dealing with crew issues.

Captain Mike's advice comes from years of seafaring around the world on power and sailboats of all sizes, and seaworthiness. As boaters, we are aware that boating can change from the serene to the chaotic in an instant.

Although some sections and content may have less appeal than others, readers should familiarize themselves with the contents and the index so that specific chapters can be

Referenced as needed… hopefully well in advance of any crisis.

As readers, it is important to understand that a work of this type is never finished, but as an author, there comes a time to get out the First Edition. As readers, this information has the potential to save a boat and crew. Thank you Captain Mike: for sharing yourself and your knowledge.

Sally C. Hass

Pilot, "Spirit of Balto"

January 3, 2008

Figure 1 – Bill & Stella Work, Building Diesel China. "So that others  **Kimley. Hard at Ducks at Zhuhai, may live."**

Preface

 THIS book is for those who go to sea, cruise aboard small boats and hunger for some adventure, just short of being in more trouble than they can get out of.

If you are going to sea, cruising in foreign waters, faraway lands, or just across into the next state, then this is where to start to learn the ropes. You can learn all the boating basics in say, five years, and spend all the rest of your life learning the rest.

This is not intended as a replacement for the usual Cruising Guides. It is simply a master book about clearance, foreign cruising, and state-to-state issues. There are phone numbers and web site links. The long URL web site links have been supplemented with "tinyurl" links that will save you much typing and possible error prone entries.[2]

The long URL versions are generally in the End Notes, marked with roman numerals[i], at the very back of the book: page 174; but before the Salvage Form (footnotes are marked with [1]).

This entire subject area is a kind of giant maze with dead ends in every direction. It is hard to find information, people to contact and get clarification, or to run down and eliminate rumors and erroneous information. Even when you can find a phone number, the resulting endless menu selections eat up phone time and sometimes disconnect. This book is intended to help you put an end to such problems.

This material is oriented towards U.S. Citizens, but I have included material that is entirely generic to citizens of other countries.

No one should completely depend on any of the information I have supplied here to stay out of trouble. Be especially wary of "jail house attorneys" that you meet in bars, frequented by yachtsmen. The rumor mill is full of experts, with a couple of year's experience, who can get you into trouble. That is why I wrote this little book. If what you need to know is not here, it is time to consult someone who is a known expert in the field. I have consulted with such experts in its preparation, and have taken precautions to prevent you from being misled.

---

[2] See Internet Resources, page 89.

There is a saying in yachting; "You, are responsible for your vessel and crew." You are now the Captain, the First Mate, the Second and the deckhand... the responsibilities and tasks that lie before you are extensive and full of details, which you can learn here, or by trial and error. The choice is yours.

You are expected to know the elementary boating skills from the bible of boating, *Chapman's Seamanship and Small Boat Handling*. If you know the material written here, inside out, you will have more knowledge than all but 1 in 10,000 average yachtsmen. Knowledge, which you can put too valuable use, to help yourself; and to train and help others.

I did not envision this as an *Encyclopedia of Foreign Clearance*. Think of it as *A Little Black Book* for yachtsmen, where Foreign Clearance, High Seas Legal Issues, State-to-State Cruising, Taxes, Registration, Numbering, Handling Emergencies, Piracy, and a myriad other little known topics can be found.

This book is not intended as a replacement for a lawyer. The topics covered are more complex than can be fully covered in even a few thousand pages. The style is informal and not a formal treatise on law. Yet, I have included numerous references to the actual Federal, or State statutes, not only so that you can do further research yourself, but also that you may be able to verify the accuracy of the material presented.

This book is not a piece of stone, a monument, only to be gazed upon. Make notes in it; fill in the margins, the back, the blank page. Don't be shy. Make corrections, or add comments to suit you. This is a working reference to keep you out of trouble, and save time, and money.

Work over this book as you would a backyard garden. Till the soil, water the plants, inspect for insects, pull up the weeds, but make something happen!

Michael Phillip Maurice. April 14, 2008

Introduction

FIRST, a history of the word *Smuggling*. The Old English appears to come from the German verb, *smeugan* (Old Norse *smjúga*) to "creep into a hole". Bootlegging is an American word associated with similar activities; it first appeared in the Omaha Herald in 1889:

> There is as much whisky consumed in Iowa now as there was before... "for medical purposes only,", and on the bootleg plan.

A bootleg refers to the long leather boots worn by cowboys in the Old West. They were used to store all manner of illicit goods, including an extra gun, a bowie knife or a flask of moonshine. Incidentally, a bootleg play in football refers to quarterback running pattern that entails making a sharp perpendicular turn around the tight end.[ii]

Non-U.S. Boats & Citizens

The material is U.S. oriented, but I have included material and links that are specific to citizens of other countries. There is a complete list of Embassy Web Sites[3], from which you can find the embassy for most countries. At least ⅔ of the book is generic to any country's cruisers.

Where there is a reference to contact a U.S. government agency, think **your** country's counterpart agency.

Even where the information is U.S. specific, this will give you insight into what other countries are doing, and with the web links you should be able to find the details that you need.

The most important document you can have when visiting the U.S. is a copy of the United States Coast Guard (USCG) Navigation Rules for International and Inland Waters (COLREGS). It contains the Bridge-to-Bridge Radio Rules, Boundary Lines, and VTS Monitoring tables. It is available as a download from the USCG web site, see footnote page 1.

---

[3] See page 105. http://tinyurl.com/35kvkv

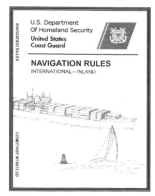

Figure 2 – COLREGs & Inland Rules

State names with abbreviations can be found on page 114. Monetary amounts are in U.S. dollars unless noted otherwise.

Footnotes

There are two types of footnotes in the book. The End Notes are numbered with Roman Numerals: i, ii, iii, iv, etc. and have been used for web URL links that take up too much space to included on each page. Footnotes numbered with Arabic numbers: 1, 2, 3, etc. are located at the bottom of the page.

Important Note

The material contained here defines what the technical, legal requirements are. Some experienced boaters will tell you that this material is nonsense. They may think so because they have never run into the problem and been fined. Nevertheless, I can assure you that the legal issues have been carefully researched.

I have provided Internet links and references to the legal underpinnings, where I could locate them. Where possible, I have included tables which indicate how a group of jurisdictions treats some specific issue, such as Titling or whatever. Where such a table does not exist, I have made an effort to note that fact.

In any event, many of these technicalities are ignored or unenforced, which is why many boaters think, "that, it's not so". I am not trying to give you advice, so much as information. What you do with it is up to you.

There is some information about Sales, Use, Excise[4], and Property[5] Taxes.[6] It is beyond the scope of this book to provide explicit information,

---

[4] http://tinyurl.com/yv4p6w

[5] http://tinyurl.com/2ckzc3

[6] http://tinyurl.com/23cz8o

to you, regarding such matters. I have included tables, to help you find such details, for your jurisdiction.

I have 50 years experience going to sea, and have packed everything I know about these topics into the material provided.

Corrections

There are many URL links, and as you may be aware, they change from year to year and can easily become obsolete. I have no simple cure for this problem. However, corrections with working links can be found at this web page on my web site. If you find that a URL link is no longer working, check the link below. If there is no update link at my web page, send an email to alert me to the situation, see Report Errors, page xix.

http://www.yachtsdelivered.com/bookpub.html

Accuracy

There is a lot of information packed into this book. There are bound to be errors either from information that was originally faulty, or from a mistake while typing or editing. I have taken precautions to assure that the information is accurate. But, even that is only true at the time of its entry into the word processor.

Regulations change and there is no substitute for the most recent info. The date and time that this document was last worked on is on page iii.

Web sites that present official information from the respective agency are the most accurate, followed by web sites prepared by secondary providers, followed by various web blogs and forums. Do not *bet the farm* on anything except sites or information that can be confirmed from the official agency concerned. In the case of tax questions, you can get a rough idea from talking to other boaters, but the only safe course is to consult a tax expert, someone who works with boating tax law. Expert at your state's taxes would be best.

Report Errors

In this document to the author at:

docerror@yachtsdelivered.com

Label Making

Get a portable label maker, such as one of the Brother[7] units or similar; use plastic, not paper label material. Use it to mark critical ship's information. Without labeling, your vessel is essentially a *one-man* boat; with which no one can properly assist you, or take over, if necessary.

Added for Completeness

Here and there I have included some bit of material, not because it was very necessary, but "for completeness". In other words, someone may ask you sometime about some obscure topic and you will recall that I included it here, *for completeness*.

---

[7] Model PT-1280, $40

Acknowledgements

Technical Advice

Duffy Bouvia. Dr. Bob Austin. Lloyd Billings (Unlimited Master, Ret.). Various contacts at: U.S. Customs and the U.S. Coast Guard.

Figure 3 – Japanese Navy Ship, Hakodate Harbor, Hokkaido Island, Japan

Section 1 – ▷ Navigation Rules

 AS you well know you cannot Smuggle Your Boat Out of Jail and that is the whole point. Since you cannot, the trick is to not get it there in the first place.

If you are reading this and think I am going to teach you how to smuggle, then you have been cheated! Which may well be your the first lesson in smuggling; it is cheating and you have become the cheatee (cheated), whereas, practicing smuggling would make you a cheater. I trust you are taking notes, as there will be a quiz!

What I will not cheat you out of, is a good read. Smuggling conjures up tales of Piracy, Rum Running, Tales of the High Seas and Dark Coves on Stormy Nights. I tell you how to handle various obscure emergencies involving the authorities, such as a collision or being arrested, and hard to find Information & Tips on clearing-in and out of foreign countries.

The Captain's Authority

The Captain's authority rests on tradition and Admiralty[8] Law. One of the most explicit; ignored elements of this chain of responsibility stems from Rule 2(a) of the COLREGS.[9]

> (2)(a) Nothing in these Rules shall exonerate any vessel, or the owner, master, or crew thereof, from the consequences of any neglect to comply with these Rules, or of the neglect of any precaution which may be required by the, ordinary practice of seaman, or by special circumstances of the case.

In summary, the Vessel is responsible to the Rules, the Owner is responsible to the Rules, the Master is responsible to the Owner and the Rules, and the Crew is responsible to the Master and to the Rules.

---

[8] http://www.admiraltylawguide.com/

[9] International Collision Regulations, U.S.C.G. Publication COMDTINST M16672.D

http://www.navcen.uscg.gov/mwv/navrules/navrules.htm

Note that crew can be held responsible for violations of the Rules. Violations by any of the parties can make them subject to civil penalties of up to $5,000 per violation.

The Captain's authority to enforce compliance with the Rules is obvious from the above. In short, the Captain's authority is absolute even in the presence of the owner. Lawful orders, which emanate from the Captain's Discretion or Authority, must be obeyed.

Failure to obey orders can result in the vessel being fined, or detained, with those aboard being arrested and jailed. This is a real possibility in the case of an accident. The captain and crew were detained briefly, but it could have been worse, over the April 2006 incident where a 62' Nordhavn went aground near Magdalena Bay, Mexico. In the case of the Earthrace boat that struck and killed some fishermen off the Nicaraguan coast in 2007, the captain and crew were held for some days and might have been jailed indefinitely.

The Captain is obligated to use force where necessary, to prevent an assault upon any person on board, or to quell a mutiny.

The Authorities of the vessel's Flag Country have jurisdiction over the vessel while on the High Seas, and may be given such jurisdiction for any acts which occur in a foreign country's jurisdiction.

Criminal violations which occur aboard a U.S. Flag vessel, on the High Seas, are subject to U.S. criminal statutes[10], with potentially significant fines and imprisonment; small craft are not exempt.

Unique COLREGS

---

[10] Federal Law applies; not the state you are from.

Canada and the U.S. have the most comprehensive set of modifications to the COLREGS. Canadian Sailing Directions generally contain these modified regulations.

http://tinyurl.com/bshm9 ⁱⁱⁱ

A number of other countries with significant maritime activity have modified regulations for their internal waters. The U.S. Inland Rules are a specific example, but the U.S. is not an isolated case. You are subject to these rules, which you may not be aware of, when in the internal waters of some foreign country. Be sure to ask the locals since there is no table by-country that I can refer you to.

See European Canals page 91.

Here is an example of the Canadian changes, those to the Safe Speed Section in Rule 6.

Safe Speed–Canadian Modifications

(c) In the Canadian waters of a roadstead, harbour, river, lake, or inland waterway, every vessel passing another vessel, or work that includes a dredge, tow, grounded vessel, or wreck shall proceed with caution at a speed that will not adversely affect the vessel, or work being passed, and shall comply with any relevant instruction, or direction contained in any Notice to Mariners, or Notice to Shipping.

(d) For the purpose of paragraph (c), where it cannot be determined with certainty that a passing vessel will not adversely affect another vessel, or work described in that paragraph, the passing vessel shall proceed with caution at the minimum speed at which she can be kept on her course.

(e) In the Canadian waters of a roadstead, harbour, river, lake, or inland waterway, every vessel shall navigate with caution, and shall comply with any relevant instruction, or direction contained in any Notice to Mariners, or Notice to Shipping where abnormal water levels, ice conditions, or a casualty to a vessel, or aid to navigation may

(i) make navigation difficult, or hazardous,

(ii) cause damage to property, or

(iii) block the navigational channel.

Variability in Laws, Regulations & Enforcement

Each country has unique issues with smuggling and the breaching of their security. For instance, in The Bahamas, it is yachtsmen bringing small boats and motors, and selling them to the locals, duty-free. There are similar problems in Turkey. As a consequence, these two countries are very sensitive and have what appear to be irrational procedures, which are an attempt to prevent these transfers from occurring.

For instance, it is prudent to mark your tender and dinghy(s) with the name of the mother vessel; as well as the state registration numbers and have copies of: the title and current registration.

There is a tremendous variation in the level of enforcement and interest shown by the local authorities. Where yachtsmen have abused the sensibilities and laws of some country, such as Turkey or The Bahamas, the result has been stepped up enforcement. Keep that in mind when you visit foreign lands. You can spoil it for those who come after you.

A History of Clearance Law

The laws were not originally designed to deal with recreational vessels. However, in many places there is only one set of laws, and recreational boats are subjected to them in an identical manner to that of large commercial vessels, see page 75.

Section 2 – ▶
Clearing

Clearing In & Out of Foreign Countries

Night Entry or Leaving

 DO not ever enter or leave, the country at night, unless you have explicit permission to do so. In other words, be in radio contact with the authorities.

There is some temptation to avoid contact by radio where you do not speak the language very well. However, night entries are likely to get you yelled at, or worse, especially countries that do not get many yachts as visitors.

Figure 4 – Curious Japanese Fishermen Meet Americans

General

The Captain is legally responsible for The Clearance. Keep the paper documents from all clearings. If done by telephone, be certain to enter the Clearance Number in your records, log book, etc. Get the Clearance Number or the name of your contact before your cell phone disconnects and you cannot find that person again.

Do not let anyone else talk to the clearance officer until you have that number. The fines for violating U.S. Customs Regulations are

$5,000 per instance and almost any tiny mistake, or lack of being able to prove The Clearance can result in this penalty.

Record the Time, Date, Location, and Clearance Number.

If you fail to hear the Clearance Number due to the conversation being prematurely terminated, call back and get one.

Especially with U.S. Customs, do not depend on anyone, not even the vessel's agent to finalize your clearance and get the number. One hour before arrival, make contact with them by phone, or whatever, and announce your intentions. Where docking, what time, how many on board, nationalities, etc.

Before you get anywhere near U.S. territory, you are well advised to have the phone number and be in contact during regular business hours with the Customs Office where you intend to clear-in. This may sound a little paranoid, but *things have changed* recently, try to be helpful.

The Customs people are just trying to do a difficult job, and they need your help. Point out that you bought this book, have read it, and applied that which you learned, in order to be helpful.

This URL leads to the reporting stations with telephone numbers for the entire U.S.

http://tinyurl.com/2vq3kr [iv]

The Outlying Areas Reporting System (OARS), presently operates in the NE States and Great Lakes Region, for details:

http://tinyurl.com/35ga92 [v]

If you cannot find a phone number to call, try these:

Seattle, Washington area: +1-800-562-5943

San Diego, California area: +1-619-685-4304

Portland, Maine area: +1-207-532-2131 ext. 255

Miami, Florida area:

+1-800-432-1216, or +1-800-451-0393

U.S. Customs – Notice to Masters

Notice to Masters of Vessels

Publication № 0000-0581

This is one of those documents you want to read, carefully, seven pages.

http://tinyurl.com/2thvzq [vi]

U.S. Customs Web Page for Travel-by-Boat Issues

Figure 5 – U.S. Customs Web Page

http://tinyurl.com/yovyb9 [vii]

U.S. Know Before-You-Go Web Pages

http://tinyurl.com/2lgggt [viii]

Visa Waiver Program

Most of the world's air carriers can set up incoming travelers to receive a visa waiver good for 90 days upon arrival in the U.S. and many other countries. This waiver is not necessarily usable for other travel across nearby borders.

For instance, you arrive by air in Canada and get your waiver, then later ride on a boat from Victoria BC over to Friday Harbor, Washington for lunch; this is presently a problem. Phone the Customs Agency office at the destination, before heading across the border, thinking that your waiver is valid for such an excursion; see Travel Visas, Appendix.

Foreign Yachts Visiting the U.S.

Anyone visiting the U.S. who is not a resident needs a Visa from the U.S. government. There are a few exemptions for residents of certain foreign countries including Canada, etc. Be sure to get the Visas ahead of time.

Consider having anyone not necessary to the operation of the boat, and having a Visa, they should enter the U.S. by some other means than with the boat: by air or surface transportation. For instance, stop in Canada or The Bahamas and have your people enter separately and join the boat after the boat has been cleared into the U.S. This may seem a bit ridiculous, but this can be a big help.

Health

Medical Clearance: sometimes a doctor, many times by one of the officials below.

Immigration

Handles issues regarding: people, their nationalities and visas, etc.

Customs

Handles Duty on items you are importing; the boat, personal, or attempts to smuggle; same.

Agriculture

Your food and produce.

Clearing In

Includes visits from Health, Immigration, Customs, and Agriculture.

Clearing Out

Immigration, Customs and Port Captain.

Liquor

Many countries including the U.S. severally limit the amount of liquor that can be brought in with the boat, and the duty on liquor is high.

Rarely Asked for Documents

Ship's Radio Station License, since you may be asked for your call sign and MMSI[11] number. In which case, you may need to prove that it is legitimate; also, your Restricted Operators Permit[12] and copy of FCC Regulations Title 47 Part 80.[13]

- Vaccination Cards.
- Clearance from Last Port, see page 26.
- EPIRB registration sticker.
- See also, page 66.

Dinghy-Tenders

Dinghy-tenders should have a registration from your home state and be sure to carry a copy of the title with your ship's papers. There is a rumor that you can just put the name of the mother vessel on the dinghy and that is sufficient; such information is wrong.

You need proof of ownership for any separate equipment of any value and a $10,000 dinghy is separate and substantial by any definition. In general, the dinghy is exempt only if it has no motor, or is used strictly to ferry the mother vessel's passengers to and from, an adjacent pier, or beach. In any event, at some level of value it should be registered and have numbers, regardless of its use. A proper dividing line might be $500, see page 78, Numbered Vessels.

Garbage – Refuse

Many countries are becoming sensitive about refuse. Here are a few guidelines.

- Separate your garbage into food, metal, paper, plastic.

---

[11] See page 100.

[12] See: FCC Web Site form № 605.

[13] Online version: select latest year, then part 80.
http://www.hallikainen.com/FccRules/

- ❏ Do not contaminate the metal, paper, or plastic with food.
- ❏ Do not use your electric garbage disposal near shore, inside 3 miles.

Pumping Holding Tanks

Some countries are requiring that yachts not pump holding tanks inside of 12 miles. The U.S. regulations allow outside of 3 miles except in a few places on the Florida and Gulf States coast's where it is 9 miles.

Secured & Sealed in a Locker

In some countries Customs will allow you to place in a locked compartment, articles such as liquor, guns, cigarettes, etc. Seals will be applied and cannot be broken until after you clear their territory.

In the U.S. you will have to supply your own seals and a Bond. Such a bond is called an International Carrier Bond. It is not clear that such a bond can be acquired for a yacht's operation, at a cost that makes sense.

If you have one of the combination locks with four wheels on the bottom[14], that you can set the combination by inserting a pin, with the lock in the unlock state; then you could have the authorities reset the combination to a number known only to them. Have the number recorded in their paperwork. Your copy should not have the number, only a reference that, the original papers have the number, to be revealed only upon clearing out. Later you will only have to have them supply the number, in order to remove the lock, no hacksaw required.

Cruising License-Permits

United States

The U.S. Customs Service will issue a Permit to Cruise U.S. Waters to a select group of reciprocating countries' flagged yachts.[15]

---

[14] Abus Marine Brass Combination Lock: 15812, $21. http://tinyurl.com/ynvg5h

[15] Title 19, Part 4.94

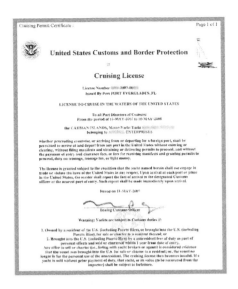

Figure 6 – Sample Cruising License

Cruising Licenses exempt pleasure boats of certain countries from having to undergo formal entry and clearance procedures (obtaining permits to proceed, as well as from the payment of entrance and clearance fees), at all but the first port of entry. These licenses can be obtained from the U.S. Customs and Border Protection Port Director at the first port of arrival in the United States. Normally issued for no more than a year, a Cruising License has no bearing on the duty owed of a pleasure boat.

Keep in mind that the requirement to *report* is not waived, just because you have a Cruising License; carefully note what the second paragraph reads. In some cases, you may be required to report only when the boat moves from one Customs District to another. Be sure to follow the instructions you are given and make a record of this in your logbook.

The districts[16] generally follow the state boundaries, but there are many exceptions. Big states often have more than one district.

If you were to stop at each state, going up or down the U.S. East Coast, you could possibly stop in more than a dozen districts between Connecticut and Virginia. In that area, you really need to watch your step if the boat is foreign flagged.

---

[16] http://www.cbp.gov/xp/cgov/toolbox/ports/

- New York has four districts; just because of its complicated commercial air and sea shipping.

- Massachusetts and Connecticut are both in the same district.

- California, Washington, Florida, and Texas each have two districts.

- Minnesota has three.

- Oregon's district includes the Washington side of the Columbia River, and Boise Idaho, all in adjacent states.

- District of Columbia and Alexandria Virginia is a single district, separate from Maryland and the rest of Virginia.

- New Jersey is spread out across several districts.
- Delaware is part of the New York district.

See Maps of Districts, page 134. Be warned, these maps are not official U.S. Customs Maps and are only a rough guide as to the boundaries of the various districts.

Successive Cruising Permits

Under-policy, upon expiration of a vessel's Cruising License, that vessel will not be issued another license until it again arrives in the United States from a foreign port, or place, and more than 15 days have elapsed since the vessel's previous Cruising License expired.

Customs Directive № 3100-06, November 7, 1988

http://tinyurl.com/3322bo [ix]

U.S. Reciprocal Cruising License Countries[17]

Vessels of the following countries are eligible for Cruising Licenses (these countries extend the same privileges to American pleasure boats). This list is subject to change, most likely by additions.

---

[17] See terms of Reciprocity page 88.

Argentina, Belgium, Finland, Honduras, Liberia, Sweden, Austria, Bermuda, France, Ireland, Netherlands, Switzerland, Australia, Canada, Germany, Italy, New Zealand, Turkey, Bahamas Islands, Denmark, Greece, Jamaica, Norway.

Great Britain, including Turks and Caicos Islands, St. Vincent (including the territorial waters of the Northern Grenadine Islands), the Cayman Islands, the British Virgin Islands, and the St. Christopher-Nevis-Anguilla Islands.

Countries by Map Area

Argentina, The Bahamas Islands, Bermuda, Canada, Honduras, Jamaica. And former British Colony Islands from above.

Austria, Belgium, Denmark, Great Britain, Greece, Finland, France, Germany, Ireland, Italy, Netherlands, Sweden, Switzerland, Turkey, Norway.

Australia, New Zealand

Liberia

A Horror Story

Read the story below of the yacht that got fined some $5,000 times eight ($40,000) for not reporting-in, while on a U.S. Cruising License.

http://tinyurl.com/325tfn [x]

Other Countries

Mexico does not issue a formal Cruising License as does the U.S. However, clearing from port to port is much simpler than in years past.

For other countries, consult local cruising guides for current information.

Length of Cruising Permits

The U.S. generally allows 12 months.

Mexico allows several years.

A more complete table will be constructed with emphasis on countries that are extremely liberal and those that are extremely restrictive.

Countries with Liberal Permit Lengths

U.S. - 12 months.

Countries with Restrictive Permit Lengths

Australia: length of the Captain's Visa.

Panama: 3 months, extensions available.

Exemption to a Formal Entry

An American owned pleasure boat arriving in the United States from a foreign port, or place, is not required to make formal entry (payment of entrance and clearance fees, etc.) provided: the vessel is not engaged in trade; the vessel has not visited any hovering vessel. Is eligible if:

1) Any vessel that has visited a hovering vessel, if the master reports arrival as required by law, and is in compliance with U.S. Customs, and Border Protection navigation laws, and...

2) Any article on board by law to be entered, or declared is reported to U.S. Customs, and Border protection immediately upon arrival. If these requirements are not met, the vessel must make formal entry with U.S. Customs, and Border Protection within 24 hours after arrival.

Provided that the vessel is American owned and American built. If foreign built, and never having been formally entered, see Vessel Never Before Entered, page 15.

Hovering Vessel

19 USC 1401(k)[18] describes a hovering vessel as:

Any vessel that is found, or kept off the coast of the United States within, or without the Customs waters, if, from the vessel's history, conduct, character, or location, it is reasonable to believe that such vessel is being used, or may be used to introduce, promote, or facilitate the introduction, or attempted introduction of merchandise into the United States in violation of U.S. laws.

---

[18] See USC Documents page 93.

Entering Without the Owner

It is hazardous to make entry, without the owner aboard, using expedited entry procedures. In other words, if the boat is not yours and you are entering the U.S., be sure to specify and use form № 1300. The boat will be given a more careful inspection, but the Captain will generally **not be responsible** for its use after entry.

If the boat was rented, and it is a private trip where the Captain was not paid by the rental company, use the expedited procedure. If the rental company supplies the Captain, use the commercial form № 1300. When there is any doubt as to the proper procedure, be sure to ask.

Entering a Foreign Built Boat

If you are returning to your own country, boats built in another country are often subject to duty. Even if there is no actual payment required, there is usually paperwork needed. In the case of a U.S. citizen bringing in a foreign built boat, even one that you recently took out of the country, Customs may require proof of the duty having been paid. Be sure you have a copy of that proof before you leave the U.S., see page 100.

Vessel Never Before Entered

In the case of an entry to the U.S. by a foreign built boat, if the boat has not ever been formally entered then it will be necessary to do so. A special Customs form may be used in some cases, but this form must be signed by the actual owner; *in person*. Otherwise, it will be necessary to have the formal entry made by a bonded, licensed, customs broker. The difference in cost is around $500.

This process is required even where no duty is due. If you are bringing in a boat never having visited, be aware of this *gotcha*!

Over 20 meters in Length

If the boat is over 20m, it comes under special regulations and is no longer considered a Motorboat. Under the FSBA of 1971[19], and its predecessors, it is technically a Motor Vessel.[20]

---

[19] See page 102.

Your FCC ship's Station License should read **SB** not SA since you are *required* to have an FCC license and to monitor channel 13, the Bridge-to-Bridge (B2B) Channel, when underway.

This B2B Channel monitoring applies to all vessels, regardless of country flag, and the person who is doing the monitoring is required to have a command of English. This requirement applies inside the U.S. 12 mile territorial sea.[21]

Yachts Over 100 Gross Tons

Any recreational boat over 100 GT is likely to be treated in a commercial class in some countries. There is no summary list for this issue.

You may be asked for the vessel's IMO number. Recreational Vessels are not issued such a number. If you are questioned about this, the IMO website will confirm it.

Commercial Versus, Recreational

One of the things to keep in mind is that in countries or ports where the authorities are unfamiliar with recreational vessels, clearing-in and out, is likely to be a hassle. As countries become accustomed to recreational boats they are streamlining procedures. However, if you get to some country where clearing is still awkward, try to be patient. Be sure to study the cruising guides beforehand, for country, or port specific information.

Notice of Arrival

24?? Hour Warning

Failure to provide warning of your approach to a new country, or port, is considered a serious issue in some countries; the larger the boat, the more serious the fines or treatment. A few countries require more than 24 hours. Countries that are touchy about this include: those **not** commonly visited by recreational vessels, and those with security concerns. Check current information for the country involved.

---

[20] http://tinyurl.com/2lhgnc

[21] See the Territorial Sea magenta line on your charts.

If you provide notice by fax, radio, or whatever, be sure to get a confirmation in writing, if possible. At the very least, a confirmation number or identification (ID) from whomever you are in contact with.

Where to Find Notice Times

The Coast Pilots for the U.S. have some information. The Sailing Directions (NGA[22], U.S. versions) do not have the information in any consistent or reliable way.

In general, it is hazardous to your pocketbook to rely on anything but current information. Only current government web sites, email, and phone calls should be relied upon.

Australia – AU

Australia cost some cruiser about $15,000 dollars for not giving a *minimum* 96 hours warning, see the story at:

http://tinyurl.com/ytta53

The solution, since they did not have a good communications system, was to have faxed the Australian authorities before departing from their last port, and getting a confirmation in writing, see Notice of Arrival.

AU Notice Requirements

96 hours notice, may be given by either —

Sending an email to yachtreport@customs.gov.au

Sending a fax to +61-2 6275-6331, or,

Phoning the Australian Customs National Communications Centre at: +61-3-9244-8973.

You will need to provide the following information

1) The name of your craft;

2) Your intended first port of arrival;

3) Your estimated arrival time;

---

[22] Formerly known as NIMA

4) Your last four ports;

5) The details of people on board including name, date of birth, nationality, and passport number;

6) Details of any illness, or disease recently encountered;

7) If you have any animals on board;

8) If you have any firearms on board.

Here is the URL to the Australian Web Page

http://tinyurl.com/2xz42j [xi]

New Zealand, Fiji, and Costa Rica are requiring 48 hours notice.

Advance notice, Wiki link.

http://tinyurl.com/3x4462

Finding Web Sites

Customs

Many other web sites can be accessed by changing the last two characters after .gov to something like "uk" for United Kingdom, etc. See page 89 for an abbreviated list.

There is another variation where the ".gov" is shortened to ".go" for instance

.customs.go.jp, for Japan.

This web site has a set of links to about 60 of the world's major customs web sites. It is not complete, not all the links work, and be warned, some of the sites are NOT government but private web sites.

World Customs, organization

http://tinyurl.com/2ktwqw [xii]

Most of the sites have an English version. The key word *English* is generally near the top of the main page. Just click on it and the page will refresh in English.

See Appendix page 138, a List of Customs Web Sites.

General Searches on Google

You can enter the string as a search in Google, for instance "customs.gov.bm" for Bermuda.

Adding the string "vessel arriving" may help to narrow the search down.

Cruisers Information

Some of the web sites have easily found information for yachtsmen and some do not.

Big Luxury Yachts

Big yachts with jet skis, many tenders, or a helicopter, generally require detail information, and most likely an agent to facilitate the arrival.

For yachts over 100 feet, or with special needs try this outfit.

http://www.c2conline.net/

Crew Issues

You can get into bigger trouble over crew than you can imagine. A few rules of thumb:

1. Have crew whose passports are issued by the country you are about to enter.
2. If not № 1 above, keep in mind, that the boat and captain are legally responsible for each and every person brought into the country.
3. This responsibility is absolute and can result in the boat and crew being detained and fined.
4. In order to be removed from this responsibility, a crewman must be removed from the crew list by the proper authorities.

The boat is responsible for crew, their expenses, medical, passport, visa, and even their travel home, or being arrested.

You will/may not be allowed to leave the country without the same crew that you entered with, unless, those crew have been officially removed from the crew list.

If you are boarded while offshore and listed crew are not on board, you may have a lot of explaining to do; be prepared!

If a crewman wants to leave, but not with you, they must be taken to immigration and have the crew list changed. Immigration will generally require that someone provide proof of how the leaving is going to occur, whether by plane, or ship (with a ticket as proof), or as crew on another yacht, etc.

If the crewman does not have the financial wherewithal to purchase a ticket out, you will be responsible. This can be a sticky situation, as you may not want them aboard but have trouble trying to get separated from them.

Be careful about taking a crewman on who may be some other boat's *castoff*. The other boat may be desperate enough to get rid of someone that you will be misled about their true nature.

A checklist of things to verify about prospective crew:

❑ Verify the passport and its expiration date.

❑ Same thing for any needed visas

❑ Have it in *writing* that they are responsible for their expenses: medical, return home travel, visas, and passport. Having it in writing, may or might *not* be of real value.

Crew Arriving to Join the Boat

It is a good policy to provide anyone coming to join the boat with a copy of the Cruising Permit, or, if not available a copy of the Ship's Document. See Parts & Materials for a Vessel In-Transit page 43.

In some countries, the U.S. being a prime example, it can help to have the crew join the boat rather than make entry into the country with the boat.

If the crew is bringing parts or equipment for the boat be careful that they have the copies of the best available documentation related to the boat: Import Permit, Cruising Permit, Ship's Document; in that order.

One Way Airfares

Most airlines will be wary of letting someone fly to a foreign country without a roundtrip ticket. Of course you can point out that you are coming back by boat, but having a copy of the Ship's Document, and or, Cruising Permit should get you over this hurdle. Like you, they can be held responsible for everyone they bring into the country.

Radio Licenses

Technically speaking, you are required to have licenses for any transmitting equipment that you have with you (Amateur/HAM, ship's, etc.). This is rarely enforced, but be prepared by asking other cruisers before you depart for the destination country.

Amateur (HAM) Radio

You can always claim that even if you have HAM gear, and no license to operate in the visiting country, that you will not transmit without permission. Keep in mind that this may not be acceptable.

However, you can always point out that since you came by boat that you need the gear to transmit while on the High Seas, whereas, those who come by land or even by air are in no position to do so, and you are, and have such a need.

Foreign Country Operation
http://tinyurl.com/25v3jy [xiii]

IARP Countries
Argentina, Brazil, Canada, El Salvador, Panama, Peru, Trinidad, and Tobago, United States of America, Uruguay, and Venezuela.

CEPT Countries
http://tinyurl.com/2y9uf4 [xiv]

The CEPT countries consist of the most of the countries of Europe, western and eastern; France includes most of her former colonies.

CB Radios

The non-standard use of radio equipment in foreign countries is almost beyond imagination. In some cases, the authorities are concerned about the diversion of your equipment to rebel groups.

In many remote areas VHF marine band equipment is used by everyone, for every purpose that you can imagine; taxis, police, travel services, grocery stores, hotels, and dive shops.

In some places where even more economy of use is needed, the locals are using CB radios. You may very well encounter small boats using CB equipment and channels, rather than VHF marine band equipment.

CB Channel 9 is generally considered the emergency channel. CB usage in Mexico without a license is reported to be legal.

In some Central American countries the local boats may be using CB, and I cannot refer you to any definitive information.

If you have a SSB HF radio, most of them will receive at the frequencies that are used in CB near 27 MHz (26.965-27.405). Be sure to read this article:

http://tinyurl.com/34xx8j [xv]

Handheld VHF Radios

In many parts of the world VHF Marine radios are used very haphazardly. These habits of use, in some countries, probably will not get you into trouble.

This is not the case in the U.S. where the *UNLICENSED* use of a VHF marine radio, handheld, or otherwise, while standing on the dock, or beach is sufficient to get you a fine for $5,000.

The chances of getting fined are not high but here is how to get one. Anyone who sees you doing it can report it. The FCC has listening posts around the country; they can pick up your transmissions.

If you get a notice of violation from the FCC you are required to respond. If you lie when responding, that is a felony; whereas, the original violation is a simple misdemeanor.

Family Service Radios (FRS) are legal in many countries, but not everywhere.

Guns

Now, here is a controversial subject. In general, these are my guidelines.

There is almost no usage of a gun in a foreign country that you will be able to justify. So, don't think about it!

If the authorities do not take them for safekeeping, lock them up yourself. Do not forget the ammunition.
See Storage Locker page 10.

If you have a concealed carry permit from your home, there is probably no harm in showing it to them.

Emphasis that you have one, not because you think it gives you a right to violate their laws, but because it demonstrates that you are *law abiding*. It is some proof that you are reliable, or your home country would not have issued it to you, and secondly that having it demonstrates your willingness to be law abiding.

After all, it is not a license to *DO* anything, it is only insurance against being arrested unnecessarily. In the U.S. the misuse of a firearm, by a concealed carry permit holder is so rare as to be considered an **endangered species**.

Mexico

Even in an *emergency* do not have guns or **ammunition** aboard, and enter Mexico without having written permission to do so. Call the U.S. State Department first, for assistance. The problem is local officials wanting to confiscate your boat.

U.S.

U.S. Residents traveling with foreign made firearms are reminded to register it with CBP[23] on a CF 4457[24] prior to taking it out of the U.S. You will need to present the firearm in person to a CBP officer in order to register it. When you re-enter the U.S., a signed CF 4457 is proof that you did not acquire the foreign made firearm abroad. If you have

---

[23] Customs & Border Patrol

[24] CF means Customs Form

the original receipt for a firearm purchased in the U.S., this can be used in lieu of a CF 4457 to demonstrate that it is American goods returned.

Figure 7 – Sunset on Japanese Fishing Boat, Kushiro City Dock, Hokkaido Island

Section 3 – ▷ Clearing Out

A Real Short... Story

 HOW many times have I been approached by smugglers wanting me to smuggle their "stuff?" It is not that I have been approached personally, but I do get yachtsmen, asking me, if I have? As if, anyone in their right mind would trust me with a million dollars worth of pot to be smuggled.

Staying out of Jail

It may seem redundant to point out, that the easiest way to stay out of jail is to just play by the rules. Here are some tips on how to know the rules (which do change), and how to avoid some unintentional snares.

One reason the yachting community is so full of rumors is that none of the information is static, and *things do change*. Most of this rumor information is in error in some respects. You need to know where to find the most recent sources for the information you need. This book is designed to help you do just that.

Checklist for Leaving the U.S.

Title or Document

- If documented, original of ship's Document in-hand.
- If state registered, original of Registration, and Certified Copy of Title.
- If foreign built, Proof of Duty Paid. If proof not available, see page 100.

Boats, which are not documented (state numbered), can be taken into Canada, Mexico, and other countries, but special precautions should be taken. For instance, a certified copy of the title would be a good idea. Also, get a clearance from U.S. Customs, form № 1300.

If you expect to return to the U.S. within the calendar year then purchase the U.S. Customs Decal[25] and put it up in the specified location.

http://tinyurl.com/l95wl [xvi]

Clearance to Foreign Port

A *Vessel Entrance or Clearance Statement*: U.S. Customs Form № 1300.[26] You will *not* need this going to Canada, or Mexico[27] but there are many other places that will require it.

http://tinyurl.com/m6qmr [xvii]

Fly the Flag of Your Country

This is not a mere formality but is very important, as it is your declaration of your country of registration and can be seen by aircraft, and other vessels. Consider it a matter of politeness.[28] [29]

Extra Copies

Hint: take many copies of certain of these documents when going international. Some countries want multiple copies of each document on every check in, and out of a port, and it is a hassle to find a copier; as well as the prices for copies sometimes are exorbitant. Scan them into your laptop, and use your own printer.

---

[25] Private Vessel Decal (30 feet, or more in length): $27.50 (U.S.) per calendar year

[26] Formerly: form №1378.

[27] There are recent reports of Cancun requiring a U.S. Clearance.

[28] See: Approached by Another Vessel, page 37

[29] Flag Etiquette: http://tinyurl.com/po8vcs, http://tinyurl.com/o9cact

Ship's Stamp

Have a rubber stamp made up with the Documentation Number and vessel name. A notary-type metal seal is fancier, and more expensive, but more impressive.

Local Currency

If possible, never enter a new foreign country without some local currency, if only enough to get you through the entry procedures that will allow you to go ashore.

Power of Attorney

See Appendix page 94.

http://tinyurl.com/2v669n [xviii]

Credit Cards

Inform your bank of your plans and obtain non-800 numbers to call.

Give someone you trust Limited Power of Attorney, just to handle credit card issues.

Picking Up/Buying a Yacht in a Foreign Country

In strict terms, the vessel is obligated to abide by the laws of the flag to which it is registered. If you buy a boat in a foreign country, changing its registration can be tricky. The boat is registered either to the country where you are buying it, or to some other country.

If it is registered where you are buying it, then you may want to leave it that way until the last port in that country from which you will be departing for home, or some other country. If it is not registered there, then it may, or may not have a Cruising License, and if not, you will have to get one if available. Nevertheless, in any event, if it has one, then you should read it over carefully, and abide rigorously to the restrictions on it; which generally specify when to report.

If you clear-out of the purchasing country with the current documentation, then when you enter the next arriving country, either use the old documentation, or, if available with newly issued documentation from flag country of your choice.

You may have difficulty with insurance while you do all this. For instance, you will need insurance perhaps, but without actually having title to the boat.

Export Controlled Products

If you have a Thermal Imager (FLIR), Night Scope, late model laptop, or desktop computers, or similar equipment, these items are subject to export restrictions. What follows is not definitive, but in general:

Do not take such equipment to any of the embargoed countries, even if you keep the equipment, and return with it. Cuba, Syria, North Korea, Libya, Sudan, and Iran are on the list of such countries. Check the current lists from the U.S. Departments: Commerce and State.

http://tinyurl.com/2sur4z [xix]

You may not require an export permit if the equipment is not taken to an embargoed country, or anyone on the lists of prohibited end users, or end uses. Such exceptions come under the **NLR** (No License Required). If you need an export permit, advice on how to go about it is beyond the scope of this book.

If the equipment is installed in the boat, cannot be removed easily, and is an insignificant part of the boat's value, then it comes under the de minimis exemption, see Definitions page 99. This does not mean that you can sell the boat with the equipment intact. In the case of FLIR equipment, contact them directly (see page 95 Contacts).

You might want to put plastic tape over the labels of components mounted on the outside that advertise the unique nature of the equipment; in order to decrease the chances of attracting unwanted attention to it. You can justify this on the grounds of security, potential theft, and vandalism.

Keep in mind that if you require any replacement parts for such products while you are out of the U.S. you may have difficulty getting such parts, or get into trouble by ordering them. Due to the variety of products that might be restricted, it is not practical to describe all the possibilities. From a yachtsman's standpoint, the likely items are the one I mentioned above, or possibly some computer software. Most anything that is restricted generally will have some warning label on the equipment and, or in the manuals.

If you are asked by the authorities, make the following claims:

- ❑ That the out of country use is, or was temporary.
- ❑ That no prohibited users, or end uses have been allowed access.
- ❑ That you have NOT sold any restricted product, while outside the country.
- ❑ That you have not taken the product to an embargoed country.
- ❑ That your use comes under the NLR.

Do not lie about any of this. It is better to depend on their good sense; that any mistake on your part was unintentional, than for them to find out, you lied. They have ways of finding out about any lie; that would astound you. It is not worth it.

In practice, the equipment that is sensitive is the night vision equipment. Do not sell it, or let any non-U.S. citizen use it, or examine it. The penalties for these infractions are severe, most likely a major fine and jail time.

The U.S. Customs boarding officer is the most likely source of trouble over restricted items. However, just because you get a pass from them does not mean a report will not be sent to some other government agency, with some action taken later by one of them.

Unfortunately, the Customs people are likely to be unfamiliar enough with your particular equipment, that, they may feel compelled to contact one of the other agencies for guidance, and you can get entangled in misunderstandings without any intent on their part.

If you have any sort of issue over such matters, make notes, with, whom you dealt, the time, and place, including their handling of the matter, and keep copies of all documents you sign, or they present to you for at least a few years. There should be no harm in showing them these guidelines, and emphasizing that you have been following them to the best of your ability.

There is no statute of limitations in these cases, or for that matter in regards to U.S. Customs. That means that whatever you have done is *laid in concrete*, and proof, and witness's can be brought to bear on you many years later.

Here is the URL to the Commerce Dept. web site:

http://tinyurl.com/33erka^{xx}

In summary, the most likely way to get into trouble would be to visit one of the embargoed countries, or sell something, such as a computer. Satellite telephones have some restrictions, check with your supplier.

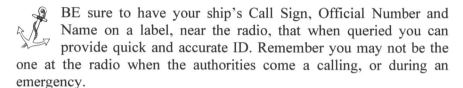

Section 4 – ➤ Offshore

Ship's Identification

BE sure to have your ship's Call Sign, Official Number and Name on a label, near the radio, that when queried you can provide quick and accurate ID. Remember you may not be the one at the radio when the authorities come a calling, or during an emergency.

Aircraft are the primary means of checking vessels within the EEZ out to 200 miles or beyond.

I would also have the Clearance Number posted near the radio, you may be asked for it. Use a small portable label maker such as: the Brother units.

Change this clearance number label as you move from country to country.

Accident Offshore, Collision, Etc

Call the U.S. Coast Guard Rescue Center as soon as possible.

U.S. West Coast - Alameda, California

☎ +1-510-437-3701

U.S. East Coast - Portsmouth, VA (Norfolk)

☎ +1-757-398-6231

They can put you in touch with the U.S. State Department if necessary. Don't be bashful, ask!

If the accident happened in International Waters do not enter a coastal country's territory or waters without first consulting U.S. authorities! In some circumstances, it might be prudent to get out of the territorial waters, if in them. In any event, you need expert advice. If the U.S. has a warship or other asset nearby, they may come and help you. Even if U.S. authorities arrest you for some reason, in many cases it is better to be in their hands than some others.

If you require assistance and the situation turns into a Salvage Operation, be sure to consult the Salvage section at the very back of the book (p. 172) for the proper form. Tear it out of the book, if necessary; that is why it is in the back!

Better yet, print out a copy from BoatUS, and fill in the blanks with your insurance company and phone number. Put this copy where you can find it easily.

Call your insurance agent as soon as possible. This last task cannot be emphasized enough!

Being Approached at Night

If you are concerned by another vessel coming around at night, especially if they are not lit, it will not hurt to transmit your identification (ID) on the VHF channel 16. Use one watt (not 25) and announce your ID with last port.

If they are dangerous, and looking for trouble, your transmission will put them off balance since they cannot be sure who else might hear the transmission, or what other steps you might be taking. If they are a warship or security vessel, you will be simply starting the process and making it clear that you have nothing to hide.

Know where you are: in the EEZ, the Contiguous Zone, or Territorial waters, and which country. See the table starting on page 153.

Safety Boarding by Coast Guard

I suggest you prepare a one-page sheet with the following information. This is just a sample so change the information to match your situation.

Notice that each item typically has the location for the item in question, as well as expiration date if applicable.

Hand this to the boarding officers on their arrival. When they see your high level of organization, they will be bowled over like a drunken sailor!

S/V Invincible – № 1,223,456

Ship's Documents – Waterproof pouch (April 30, 2010), Plastic Box.

Preferred Mortgage – Ship's Document.

Most Recent C.G. boarding sheet – Ship's Document.

Oregon State Papers (213,546) – Ship's Document. Sticker, Port Pilothouse

C.G. Aux. Inspection (2006), sticker on Port Pilothouse

Flares – With ship's Document. Expire November. 2008.

Fire Extinguishers (5 – B1) – One forward cabin, 2 main cabin, 2 pilot house.

Life Jackets – Main Cabin (4).

Throwable Type IV Horseshoe & Cushion.

Oil, Garbage Placards – Inside of Outside Pilothouse Door.

Garbage Plan – With ship's Document.

EPIRB registration sticker on EPIRB – Stb. Side Pilothouse. 1-15-2009.

FCC ship' Station License. WWW1234. Ship's Documents. 12-31-2015.

FCC Operator's Permit. Permit № 123,456.

Ship's Logbook. Stb. Side near helm.

Rules of the Road – With Flares.

Horn – Forward Outside of Pilothouse Windows.

Head Located Forward Cabin. No Holding Tank. ElectroScan Unit.

Masthead Light – Front of Main Mast, 30 feet above deck.

Stern Light – On stern.

Red/Green Running Lights – Bow Pulpit.

Tri-Color Light – Top of Main Mast.

Bailing Bucket – Engine Bilge.

Bilge Pads – Forward Cabin.

Documentation Number – Welded in Hull, Main Cabin, forward end overhead hatch.

Ship's Name – On Stern, Bow.

Extra Flares – Parachutes, Smoke, Handheld – Main Cabin (not current).

Spare Air Horn – Pilothouse.

Boat's Documentation – Forward Cabin.

Bridge Clearance. 50 feet approx.

Near Shore Cruising Obstacles

Many of the world's coastlines, especially those in what amounts to protected seas, such as the Sea of Japan, are utilized for extensive fish-eries. For instance, it is a bad idea to run within three miles of Japan especially at night; as there are numerous traps, nets, and other obstacles. The raft in the picture is about 20 feet long and sticks up about 2 feet. In general, the Sailing Directions[30] for the area will have notes concerning these obstacles; these notes cannot be completely relied upon.

Figure 8 - Japanese Bamboo Raft "Float"

[30] See: NGA page 93

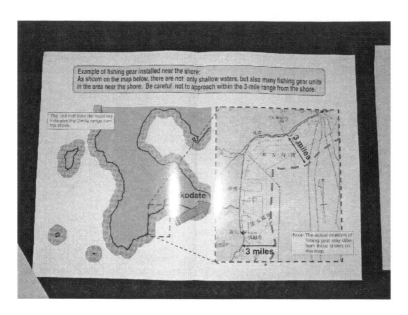

Figure 9 - Map of local hazards, Hakodate Japan

Emergency Help

U.S. Coast Guard Search & Rescue Centers

U.S. West Coast - Alameda California

☎ +1-510-437-3701

U.S. East Coast - Portsmouth VA (Norfolk)

☎ +1-757-398-6231

(Pencil in your own emergency phone numbers here)

U.S. Embassy or State Department

The contact phone numbers here may not answer quickly. If you have a time sensitive emergency, where seconds count, call the U.S. Coast Guard Search & Rescue Numbers.

Consular duty personnel are available for emergency assistance 24 hours a day, 7 days a week, at U.S. embassies, consulates, and consular agencies overseas, and in Washington, D.C.

To contact the Office of Overseas Citizens Services located in the U.S.

During business hours Mon–Fri:

0800 – 2000 EST

0300 – 1500 GMT

 +1-888-407-4747

Or after hours:

 +1-202-647-5225

Contact information for U.S. embassies, consulates, and consular agencies overseas may be found at:

http://tinyurl.com/36stpz [xxi]

Keep in mind that there are U.S. agents, and representatives, in places you would hardly imagine; Havana Cuba for instance. And, even where there are no officials, the U.S. often has contacts in other embassies that will come to your aid if asked.

Piracy

IMB Piracy Reporting Centre

Kuala Lumpur, Malaysia.

24 hour Anti Piracy HELPLINE:

 +60-3-2031-0014

U.S. Citizens While in Foreign Countries

The U.S. State Department can assist you in ways that you can hardly imagine.

- Arrange to get you access to your funds.

- Help from friends, or relatives, etc.

- Replace a stolen passport in as little as 24 hours.

If you think you *might* be arrested, contact U.S. authorities in advance, and ask to have your situation passed to the State Department.

If you are arrested, immediately ask to speak to a consular officer at the nearest U.S. Embassy or Consulate. Under international agreements, the U.S. Government has a right to provide consular assistance to you, **upon your request**. If your request to speak to your consul is turned down, keep asking—politely, but persistently. For information on how consuls assist American arrestees:

http://tinyurl.com/2sr5pm [xxii]

Search & Rescue Insurance

http://tinyurl.com/38svbs xxiii

Registering Beacons

EPIRB – 406 MHz

An EPIRB should be registered with the country where it was purchased. Each unit contains a country code, and only units with a U.S. code can be registered with NOAA.

http://tinyurl.com/397u9j [xxiv]

Australia – AMSA

For a beacon to be registered in Australia all the following criteria must be met:

- ❏ The beacon must be coded with the Australian country code 503;
- ❏ The owner must be an Australian resident, or company; and;
- ❏ The primary nominated 24-hour contact should be in Australia.

If you meet the above criteria, get and fill out the registration form, and send to AMSA by email, facsimile, or mail. Contact details are included on the registration form.

Residents of other countries, buying beacons in Australia, should have the beacon coded and registered with their country of residence.

http://tinyurl.com/2wfhrq [xxv]

Other SAR Centers

UK Falmouth Rescue

☎ +44-1326-317575

Email:

falmouthcoastguard@mcga.gov.uk

UK Beacon Registration

http://tinyurl.com/3bhx2c xxvi

EPIRB – 121.5 MHz

Overhead satellites no longer pick up these EPIRBs, but nearby search aircraft or ships can.

High Seas Law

Approached by Another Vessel

RIGHT OF APPROACH, and VISIT

As a general principle, vessels in international waters are immune from the jurisdiction of any nation other than the ship's flag nation.

See Territorial, Contiguous & EEZ Claims Tables to determine if you are in International Waters, page 153.

However, under international law, a warship, military aircraft, or other duly authorized ship, or aircraft may approach any vessel in international waters to verify its *nationality*. Unless the vessel encountered is itself a warship or government vessel of another nation, it may be stopped, boarded, and the ship's documents examined, provided there is reasonable grounds for suspecting that it is:

1. Engaged in piracy (see paragraph 3 S).

2. Engaged in the slave trade (see paragraph 3.6).

3. Engaged in unauthorized broadcasting (see paragraph 3.7).

4. Without nationality (see paragraphs 3.11.2.3, and 3.11.2.4).

5. Though flying a foreign flag, or refusing to show its flag, the vessel is, in reality, of the same nationality as the warship.[31]

This is a powerful argument for flying your Country's flag.

The procedure for ships exercising the right of approach and visit is similar to that used, in exercising the belligerent right of visit and search, during armed conflict described in paragraph 7.6.1, see Article 630.23, OPNAVINST 3120–.32B, and paragraph 2.9 of the U.S. Coast Guard's MLEM for further guidance.[32]

In summary, any nation's warships can approach to verify your identity. They may not board you except with cause as specified in items 1–5, or if granted by your vessel's flag country. If they attempt to board, you are entitled know the reason. If you are alarmed, you would be within your rights to use your communications equipment to call for advice from your country's authorities, such as the USCG.

Tactics for Right of Innocent Passage

- Avoid anchoring, if possible.

- If you anticipate being forced to anchor, attempt to communicate with the state whose waters you are transiting.

- Give them fair warning from your last port of call, if possible. Such warning consists of the usual ship, and persons on board information.

- Get and supply a *Clean Bill of Health*, even a letter from the Port Captain stating the apparent health of you and your crew is useful.

- Advise that you will take the steps described below, *if forced to anchor*.

---

[31] Fly the Flag of Your Country p.26

[32] COMDTPUB P5800.1

If Forced to Anchor

- To advise the local state by best means, radio, email, etc.

- To not go ashore.

- To not allow anyone on board, not already on board.

- To not allow trading, or physical contact with other vessels, or the locals.

Ask for provisional clearance to anchor, go ashore, to take on fuel; based on the information you have supplied. It may, or may not be granted, but there is no harm in asking. But, be sure to emphasis that if such privileges are granted, that you will not abuse them, and if not granted that you will not violate the restrictions, in any case.

Whether anchoring, or not, offer to provide by radio, once a day (?) your location, course, and speed, if so requested.

Provide these assurances in English, French, Spanish, German, or possibly some other language.

Some countries (states) are very fussy about this, and some not. Australia & Chile are very strict, French Polynesia is much less so, but this can change without much warning.

Archipelagic Countries

Antigua, The Bahamas, Cape Verde, Comoros, Grenada, Jamaica, Indonesia, Maldives, Philippines, Principe, Sao Tome, and Vanuatu.

Countries with Islands, Part of an Archipelagic Group.

Fiji, New Guinea, Seychelles, Solomon Islands, and Tonga.

Table of Archipelagic States

http://tinyurl.com/36kwck

Countries bordering Straits

Canada, U.S., Russia, Japan, Turkey, Spain, Gibraltar, Morocco, Malaysia, China, Taiwan, Turkey, Greece, England, France, Malaysia, Sumatra, India, and Sri Lanka.

http://tinyurl.com/2tj2hd [xxvii]

Major straits in the world:

- ❑ Bass Strait, lies between mainland Australia, and Tasmania. Connects the Indian Ocean with the Pacific Ocean.

- ❑ Bering Strait between Alaska, and Siberia. Connects the Pacific, and Arctic Oceans.

- ❑ The Bosporus and the Dardanelle's. Connects the Mediterranean, and the Black Sea.

- ❑ Strait of Dover, between England, and France. Connects the North Sea with the English Channel.

- ❑ Strait of Gibraltar, the only natural passage between the Atlantic Ocean, and the Mediterranean Sea.

- ❑ Strait of Hormuz. Connects the Persian Gulf, and the Oman Sea; Persian Gulf oil is shipped to the world.

- ❑ Strait of Magellan. Connects the Atlantic and Pacific Oceans north of Tierra del Fuego.

- ❑ Strait of Malacca, lies between the peninsula of Malaysia, and the Island of Sumatra. Connects the Indian Ocean with the South China Sea (one of the highest-volume shipping lanes in the world).

- ❑ Palk strait, between India, and Sri Lanka, the location of Ram Sethu

- ❑ Taiwan strait, between Mainland China, and Taiwan

The trick in innocent transit is to make sure that you are transiting; not merely using a subterfuge to hide your intention to leisurely voyage from anchorage to anchorage.

Keep the following guidelines in mind.

- ❑ Maintain a log: dates, and times of anchorage, times on passage. An electronic log, from your track log should be adequate. This assumes that you can demonstrate the time of each track entry.

- ❑ Do not create the appearance of violating the customs of innocent passage. You may be over-flown by an aircraft and photographed at any time.

Section 5 – ▷ Travel Documents

 CRUISERS should insist on extra pages for their passport. This should be done at the time of original issue. If you do not have the extra pages, get it done at the first opportunity. You will need these pages if you visit many small countries, one after the other, as in the Caribbean.

  Be sure to have extra passport photos, either for a passport renewal, or replacement, or for Visa applications.

The U.S. Government *may* allow a second passport to be issued, concurrent with another valid one, if you have a travel problem where the visa sticker or stamps, for say Israel, would prevent you from getting entry to certain countries which exclude tourists that have, or will visit Israel; as it is not an isolated case, Cyprus has similar problems.

If you are going to use this two passport trick; be sure to keep the non-used one well out of sight; when crossing a border where it could prove embarrassing and be prepared to explain it at crossings where you are not hiding it. Having two passports is sure to arouse questions.

Passport Renewals

Be sure to read the material regarding Travel Visas as you may want to renew before getting a visa. Visas expire with the passport.

Travel Visas

A visa expires on its expiration date, or the expiration of the passport, whichever, comes first. Some countries do not designate a visa expiration date (Australia does this with business visas under their ETA program), in which case the visa expires with the passport's expiration.

This fact could be useful to you; it might make it worthwhile to renew your passport, even if it is not within a year of more of expiration, country dependent.

For U.S. Citizens

http://www.travisa.com/travelvisa.htm

or

http://tinyurl.com/2lb47x

http://www.visa4you.net/index.htm

or

http://tinyurl.com/2l3rg8

Notes: about half of all countries require a visa. From a cruiser's standpoint, the ones that are the most troublesome are Australia, Brazil, the USA and Indonesia.

You cannot get a visa, or enter most countries if your passport is within six months of expiration. For U.S. Passport holders; also make sure you have enough room in the passport for the visa sticker, at least one page (pages 22, 23, 24 cannot be used for visas). A passport that is filling up can have pages added, but requires sending the passport to the passport office.

As a general rule you should get extra passport pages if you have four or fewer visa pages left. It generally takes about two weeks to send in your passport and get it back with the extra pages sewn in.

For NON-U.S. Citizens

http://www.travisa.com/nonuscitizen.asp

or

http://tinyurl.com/2rvvqo

Visa Waiver Program (VWP)

http://tinyurl.com/3bln5e [xxviii]

Be aware that the VWP is not usable if you enter by sea or by air unless it is by a commercial carrier, and one that is a participant in the program. This eliminates us yachtsmen. I have included the information only for completeness.

Electronic Travel Authority ETA

http://tinyurl.com/35uyeo [xxix]

See Current Information page 93.

Carnet

Carnets are "Merchandise Passports." They are international customs documents that simplify customs procedures for the temporary importation of various types of goods. In the U.S., two types are issued: ATA and TECRO/AIT Carnets; the latter is used only for Taiwan.

ATA Carnets ease the temporary importation of **commercial samples (CS)**, **professional equipment (PE)**, and goods for **exhibitions and fairs (EF)**. They facilitate international business by avoiding extensive customs procedures, eliminating payment of duties and value-added taxes (minimum 20% in Europe, 27% in China), and replacing the purchase of temporary import bonds.

The USCIB issues the ATA Carnets for U.S. businesses. It may be practical for yachtsmen to use this. The fee is $200-330, plus a bond of about 40% of the material to be covered. The bonds generally cost about 1%. This translates into a cost of about $200, plus $40 for a $10,000 Carnet; and about $300 for $20,000. A Carnet is issued for one year. Details on filing, where to purchase the bond, and time to acquire may be found at the USCIB web site:

http://www.uscib.org/

Bond Information

http://www.merchandisepassport.org/

Keep in mind that as far as I know, no one in the yachting community has ever used a Carnet. However, there does not appear to be any reason why one could not and the use of the Carnet is expanding. This is just one more trick in the bag of tricks that may prove useful to you.

Parts & Materials for a Vessel In-Transit

This is a very complicated topic, and you need current information which is best gotten from local cruisers; ask around.

Anything which can be sent by mail, and marked **Vessel In-transit**, accompanied with an *Invoice* on the outside of the package, has a good a chance of avoiding being held up by Customs.

The best way to get parts is to have someone hand-bring them to you. A copy of the ship's Document in their possession, or a copy of any other proof that will convince the authorities is a good idea; a letter from the vessels owner, a Carnet, a Temporary Import Exemption Certificate (Mexico issues these), etc. See also, Duty Free Ports, page 157.

Be sure to read: Crew Arriving to Join the Boat, page 20.

Section 6 – ▷
State-to-State

Cruising Reciprocity Issues

⚓ DOCUMENTED vessels without a state registration in full force-and-effect; must also obtain a STATE registration, and display the validation decal on the vessel, when using some state's waters. Florida is one such state, to be posted on the Port Side. In Florida there is – *NO grace period*!

This situation will only occur if your home state does not require registration[33] of documented vessels, or you have been away long enough that you have not been renewing your registration. The evidence of registration is the State Decal.

- Title, Register, and Number all your dinghies.

Search for current information using:

RECIPROCITY NONRESIDENT VESSEL

In Google Search add the state name, to narrow the search.[34]

---

[33] See: Phone Numbers, Reciprocity, Decals: page 122.

[34] Searching under "RV" can be a useful topic for Yachtsmen.

Documented or State Registered (Numbered) Vessels

If staying more than a visited state's maximum (generally 60 days minimum), then register with the visited state's authority. Strictly construed this would include all the dinghies, even yachts from Foreign Flag countries. See definition: *State of Principle Use* page 101, also Reciprocity page 122.

There is no consistency concerning whether State Numbering is only done in conjunction with issuance of a Title.

The issue as whether you have to obtain a new Title is unclear. Documented vessels are not going to be issued a title. For State Registered vessels, in practical terms it may not be possible to obtain a title if you are not a resident of the state. This particular tiny issue cannot be determined except by consulting the administrator of the state involved.

There is no published table, which indicates each state's policy regarding *short-term* title transfers (State by state information **not** available in table form).

Cost of registration

Compendium of All U.S. States
U.S. Master Sales and Use Tax Guide 2007: $85. CCH Tax Law Editors

http://tinyurl.com/2qlfve [xxx]

Partial, Online Copy at Google of 2005, U.S. Master Sales, and Use Tax Guide (not all pages online)

http://tinyurl.com/2978jw [xxxi]

Live Aboard

Do not use the term *Live-Aboard* when describing your status, when registering with marinas, insurance, or governmental agencies, or their agents; use: *full time cruiser*.

State Tax & Registration Issues

Note that the information about taxes, etc. in this section is oriented towards visiting other states. It is incomplete in terms of the information you will need to address these issues in the state where you reside; although the phone numbers, and offices that you will need to contact are the same.

Tax Definitions:

- Sales, a tax on Transfers of Title, except where exempted; one time.
- Use, a tax In-Lieu of Sales Tax; one time.
- Excise, generally some small amount of the vessels worth, such as half of one percent; once a year.
- Property, some states do not include boats in the property tax system. This tax is generally a local (county and, or city) tax, once a year.

Registration, Titling, Numbering

The boat is subject to this, where *Principally Used*; not necessary until minimum 60 days (six months in some states). Numerous exemptions see page 122.

Marine Title has an excellent, but incomplete site

http://tinyurl.com/2nwvab [xxxii]

Most states have Sales, or Use Taxes. Some have Property Taxes, a few have Excise Taxes.

The major problem with trying to produce a property tax table by state is that the tax is usually a local jurisdiction tax, rather than a statewide tax.

The table on page 124, is correct in regards to boats. It is not true in regards to property tax on other kinds of property, including airplanes.

http://tinyurl.com/2jxr3q [xxxiii]

As far as registration is concerned, the safest bet is to have registration from some state whether you are Documented, or Foreign Flagged. It is not clear where that registration would best be done.

Detail state-by-state registration information

http://tinyurl.com/3d7vov [xxxiv]

This is a summary listing of State Numbering requirements for visiting boats. Period of time for reciprocity[35]; whether documented vessels required to be registered.

http://tinyurl.com/3bzb8q [xxxv]

National Association of State Boating Law Administrators

Titling & Numbering

A book for $15,

http://tinyurl.com/2k7v2f [xxxvi]

Summary of 50 State Boating Issues

Latest online edition is 2001, includes U.S. Territories, excellent reference.

http://tinyurl.com/2ktr7o [xxxvii]

Reference Guide to State Boating Laws

Table 3-8 listed by states, requiring numbering, registration, or titling. Penalties see table 3-7.

State Decals: lost, damaged, or removed for maintenance can generally be replaced for a small fee. Contact your state of issuance.

Internet Discussions of Tax Issues

Florida seems to have the best web presence of any state, and I have included links to their material, as the pages are quite educational.

Florida

http://www.cruisersnet.net/index.php?categoryid=42

http://tinyurl.com/2r4k3l

or

http://www.irbs.com/lists/trawlerworld/9906/0560.html

or

http://tinyurl.com/3c8p4p

---

[35] See page 122

Sales and Use Taxes

http://tinyurl.com/3y3cqx ^{xxxviii}

Vessel Registration, Titles, Numbering

http://www.hsmv.state.fl.us/dmv/vslfacts.html#1

or

http://tinyurl.com/2qjca8

Florida has a Sojourners Permit, form HSMV № 87244 for use by Out-of-State Residents who need registration when staying beyond 90 days.

U.S. Documentation Issues

Pacific Maritime Title

Molly Holden, Manager
655 NE Northlake Way
Seattle, WA 98105

 +1-206-632-4668

 +1-206-632-4673

Section 7 – ▷ Pilotage

U.S. Pilotage Requirements for Foreign Flag Yachts

In general, the U.S. Coast Pilots state that: "All Foreign Flag Vessels" require a pilot. The Coast Pilot № 7 for 1957 reads "all vessels". It appears that sometime since 1957 The Pilots have been changed to exclude *U.S. Flag* Yachts. A foreign flag yacht can satisfy the requirement by having a First Class Pilot from the local pilots association, or by employing a USCG licensed master, or mate[36], see: Acting as Pilot page 54.

This business of requiring a pilot aboard for Foreign Flag yachts has never been enforced, except perhaps very haphazardly, as it obviously was never enforced for domestically flagged yachts in years past.

Some places on the U.S. East Coast only require a pilot on vessels with more than 9 foot of draft.

---

[36] COMDTPUB P16700.4 NVIC 8 - 94

Alaska and Washington have special rules for Foreign Flag yachts, other states may have as well. Consult The Coast Pilot for each state under the heading "Pilotage". It will be found near the beginning of the section for the state of interest, see State of Washington, page 51.

The argument for requiring a pilot is that safety is involved. The counter argument is that today's yachts are so much safer than in the past, with GPS, electronic chart plotting, and radar, that the size of vessel that justifies a Licensed Pilot should not include most yachts, regardless of Flag.

Washington State Pilotage Waters

All foreign flag yachts, (except Canadian[37]) require a licensed pilot to be aboard. Exemptions are granted to certain vessels less than 200 feet long; the charge for an exemption starts at $300 US.

Pilotage: Strait of Juan de Fuca and Puget Sound

> (79) Pilotage is compulsory for all foreign vessels, and - U.S. vessels engaged in foreign trade. Pilotage is optional for U.S. vessels engaged in the coastwise trade – with a federally licensed pilot on board (Coast Pilot 7, 2007 edition).

Pilotage waters are those: east of Port Angeles, and includes the San Juan Islands.

WAC 363-116-360 Exempt vessels

> (1) Under the authority of RCW 88.16.070, application may be made to the board of pilotage commissioners to seek exemption from the pilotage requirements for the operation of a limited class of small passenger vessels, or yachts, which are not more than five hundred gross tons (international), do not exceed two hundred feet in length, and are operated exclusively in the waters of the Puget Sound pilotage district, and lower British Columbia. For purposes of this section, any vessel carrying passengers for a fee, including yachts under charter where both the vessel, and crew are provided for a fee, shall be considered a passenger vessel.

---

[37] Can confirm Canadian.

Pilotage & British Flagged Vessels

The Treaty of 1846, between Great Britain, and the U.S. guaranteed vessels of both nations travel in the disputed areas of British Columbia, and the Columbia River.

Article I

Provided, however, That the navigation of the whole of the said channel, and straits, south of the forty-ninth parallel of north latitude, remain free, and open to both parties.

It would **appear** that all vessels of the former British Empire[38] enjoy the rights specified in the treaty; this would include Canadians, Australians, UK, etc.

In any event, here is the email from the Washington State Pilotage Commission, April 2008.

> Like a lot of treaties of the time, the "Oregon Treaty of 1846" was drafted, and signed by people who had little information on the geography of the area they were dividing up.
>
> The dispute over what was the "main channel" where the border line was established led to a war, with both British, and American forts being built on San Juan Island to fight if necessary to establish whether the line was on the east, or west side of San Juan Island.
>
> Fortunately, the only casualty was a farmer's pig, shot by a soldier of one of the garrisons.
>
> Anyway, the treaty guarantees vessels of both nations free travel in the channels through the San Juans, and the Strait of Juan de Fuca.
>
> Technically, free travel on Admiralty Inlet south of Port Townsend might not be guaranteed by the Treaty, but Washington has exempted Canadian vessels "engaged exclusively in the coasting trade on the west coast of the continental United States ... and/or British Columbia" from compulsory pilotage on Puget Sound, and Grays Harbor.
>
> I don't know that the term "coasting trade" has been defined as not including yachts, but it would create a huge international incident, and economic disruption in the local pleasure boat industry if we claimed it did not -- there aren't very many Canadian yachts that cruise the U.S.

---

[38] http://en.wikipedia.org/wiki/British_Empire

side, but thousands of U.S. yachts cruise the Canadian waters every year without taking pilots.

The treaty is reprinted at:

`http://www.ccrh.org/comm/slough/primary/ort reaty.htm`

Foreign Flag Yachts & Pilotage

Since the requirement for a pilot has historically been unenforced, you can make a case that enforcement against your vessel is discriminatory. First, on the basis that there is no credible difference in safety between domestic and foreign yachts, and secondly that it was unnecessary for domestic yachts, even at the time that it was technically required back in the 1950's.

Unless you want to make a court case out of it, you may not get very far with this argument, but it is a valid argument. In the meantime, if you do not want to be singled out, the only steps you can take are to keep a low profile. Do not fly your foreign flag, and stay out of the commercial traffic areas, where you might be noticed. Avoid transmitting AIS information.

There is one other possible line of attack if you intend to cruise in the U.S. for a year or more: to have the boat State Registered & Numbered in the U.S. If you do that, you avoid all the Customs Cruising License issues: clearing and reporting, and the state pilotage problems.

Whereas, a Numbered boat can be owned by a foreign national, it cannot be documented in the U.S. unless the owner is a U.S. Citizen. In which case if the ownership is wholly by U.S. Citizens then you could transfer the registration from foreign to U.S. and back later, if you wanted.

If you register the boat U.S., then you will be subject to U.S. Coast Guard Inspections, and will have to have life jackets, and other equipment with USCG approvals. The expense of a few life jackets and a life ring may be a small price to pay to avoid all these other hassles. However, there is one major issue left, and that is duty on the boat. If it was built outside the U.S. then it may be subject to duty or require a bond.

Renting, or Chartering a U.S. boat is one more way of bypassing the foreign flag problem.

A History of Pilotage

The states were given power to regulate foreign commerce, but not interstate commerce, at about the time of the original forming of the Federal Government. A federal pilot can pilot U.S. flag vessels, but is not empowered to do so on foreign flag vessels, unless state statute provides for it.

The Coast Pilots do not always make it clear whether a Federal Pilot is authorized to Act as Pilot, in the case, where the state has jurisdiction.

Acting as Pilot

There are two tiers of Federal Pilots: First Class, and "Acting as Pilot". See page 88 which empowers USCG licensed individuals to "Act as Pilot". Vessels over 1600 tons require a First Class Pilot, and a discussion of that is beyond the scope of this book.

In other words, foreign flag recreational boats do not have to have a First Class Pilot from the local pilots association in, order to satisfy the legal requirements for a Federal Pilot.

Unfortunately, the acting as pilot provision may not be useful in many state cases, and it may be difficult to determine from the Coast Pilot what the situation is.

Compulsory Pilotage, Foreign Yachts - U.S. West Coast

Port	Commercial	Foreign	Exempt	Fee
Alaska		>65ft	?	
Puget Sound		All	No	
Grays Harbor		All	?	
Col. River		Rec.>100ft	?	
Yaquina Bay		All	?	

Port	Commercial	Foreign	Exempt	Fee
Coos Bay		All	?	
Humboldt Bay		Registry, only		
San Francisco		All	Yes	
Monterey Bay		All	Yes	
Port Hueneme	300gt	>300gt		
Los Angeles	300gt	All	?	
Long Beach	300gt	All	Yes	Yes
San Diego	300gt	All	?	
Alaska		20m	??	

Notes:

Alaska: complicated consult Coast Pilot (CP).

Commercial, if over xxx gross tons, included only for completeness, but not verified.

Exempt, if you have a federal pilot. Verify in CP for latest information as the states can change this with little warning.

Fee charged even if pilot not employed. Avoid Long Beach side of harbor.

Puget Sound pilotage waters include the Strait of Juan De Fuca and the San Juan Islands.

Section 8 –
U.S. Laws

Ship's Station Licenses & Operator Permits
A Summary of the FCC Rules

Voluntary & Bridge-to-Bridge (B2B) Yachts

From Title 47 Part 80 of the CFR, page 62. Also, see definitions below for RP, MP, SA, SB, etc.

Going International	Ship's License, and Operator Permit Required (80.165)
Over 20 meters	License & Permit Required, same above (80.163) (B2B). No longer a voluntary ship; requires **SB** license instead of SA.
MP	Required for Teletype (Sail Mail), also if SSB over 400 watts PEP. (80.165)
	Not for HAM Winlink. HAM General needed for Winlink, roughly equivalent to MP.
	Stan Honey at SailMail reports that the FCC advised him that the MP license was NOT required for SailMail. However, the table associated with 80.165 is explicit. I have no verification from the FCC in regards to this issue.
RP	Required for SSB, Inmarsat, or VHF (VHF only if going international, or, over 20 meters). Not for Iridium, or Globalstar.
SA	Ship's station license where a radio is not required (voluntarily equipped) ($160, 2008, also SB)

SB	Compulsory ship's station license where a radio *is* required, as where over 20 meters, and subject to the B2B requirements
MP	Marine Operator Permit: $60, lifetime, requires test ($25–50)
RP	Restricted Operator Permit: $60, lifetime, no test. MP, or higher may be substituted.
FRN	FCC Registration Number (your ID with the FCC)
FCC	Federal Communications Commission
DSC	Digital Selective Calling, requires MMSI
MMSI	Marine Mobile Service Identity number, 9 digits
International	Docking foreign, or communicating with foreign coast. Not high seas or innocent passage travel.
Associated Ship	Hand held units used with mother ship. Not allowed to communicate with other vessels.
CFR	U.S. Code of Federal Regulations, non-static laws.
USC	U.S. Code, laws of the U.S., mostly static.

Note: FCC fees may have changed.

Teletype Transmissions includes Narrow Band Printing, and Fax.

Maintenance of Watch (80.309, 80.304–310)

Monitoring of Channel 16 not required if DSC monitoring of channel 70. (80.310)

Use of associated ship's portable units (80.115)

Change of Address in FRN does NOT change address in other licenses associated with that FRN.

Digitizing of FCC data is changing the way in which the FCC can identify errors in applications, and licenses. Assume that eventually they will be able to identify, and cross check the data from all your licenses. Whether there would be fines associated with such errors is hard to know at this time. But, it would be a good idea to take care with filling-in the blanks.

FCC has been conducting blanket audits of Wireless Licenses; eventually they may get around to ships.

FCC ship's Station Licenses are required to be cancelled when selling the boat to which it is associated. See the note at the bottom of the FCC ship's license "47USC309".

Installations

Installation of VHF or radar to be conducted by, or under supervision of ship's station licensee, if not a Licensed Operator (80.177), Licensed Operator required on Compulsory Ship (SB). SSB installations require an FCC licensed technician (80.169). Note: 169 is being interpreted by the user community as not requiring a licensed technician, this may not be correct.

Bridge-to-Bridge Regulations (B2B)

Subpart U, (80.1001–1023).

Subpart U is not in the COLREG book and is not widely known. This applies to vessels over 20 meters; which becomes a Compulsory Equipped Vessel, subject to watch, log, and inspection requirements.

Compulsory Ship Inspections (80.59)

External antenna required (80.1017)

Testing of radio required (80.1023)

Handheld may be used (80.143(c)), but only if not otherwise required to use VHF. Note: cannot see who could use this exemption.

Not required to monitor channel 16 if in a VTS, and monitoring the VTS channel (must be monitoring B2B channel at same time (80.148 (a), (b))).

Call on B2B channel subject to procedures in (80.331)

Inspection, and Logging, per (80.409, .1005)

Great Lakes

Applies to over 20 meters; not covered here. Subpart T (80.951)

Summary

Certain Subparts do not apply to Voluntary Yachts: Subparts J–S, and W. Subpart U is the B2B regulations, applies if over 20 meters, which then is **not** a voluntary equipped vessel.

Online Updating: FCC & EPIRB Information

New & Lost Passwords can be taken care of online.

For FCC need your FRN, and Password.

For EPIRB need beacon ID, and Password.

Ship's Station, Operator Licenses, and HAM can be Renewed, and Updated Online; can also be applied for (not HAM, or MP, and above which require a test).

EPIRB registration can be started & updated online.

Online Access to the FCC Part 80 Sections can be reached by way of the following URL Template.

Change "SECTION=1", to the correct section number.

For instance, 80.165, as "SECTION=165" substituted below.

http://frwebgate.access.gpo.gov/cgi-bin/get-cfr.cgi?TITLE=47&PART=80&SECTION=1&TYPE=TEXT

For example [xxxix]:

http://frwebgate.access.gpo.gov/cgi-bin/get-cfr.cgi?TITLE=47&PART=80&SECTION=165&TYPE=TEXT

Then enter the URL in your web browser.

U.S. EPIRB registration is located at: http://www.sarsat.noaa.gov/

The FCC is at: http://wireless.fcc.gov/uls/index.htm?job=home

Select "New Users" if you do not have a FRN.

Select "Online Filing" to apply for, or update a license.

Falsifying data supplied to the FCC is a serious matter (in USC, no reference)

The USC contains the mainly static portions of U.S. Law, and the CFR contains the material that is more often changed. For instance, Title 47 of both the USC, and CFR contains Telecommunications laws, and regulations. Likewise, Title 33 contains Shipping.

U.S. Laws of Interest to Recreational Yachtsmen

Summary of U.S. CFR [39]

Title 19 U.S. Customs: Parts 4, 148, 161, 162, 171

- ❑ 4. Vessels in foreign, and domestic trades[40]

- ❑ 148. Personal declarations, and exemptions

- ❑ 161. General enforcement provisions

- ❑ 162. Inspection, search, and seizure

- ❑ 163. Record keeping

- ❑ 171. Fines, penalties, and forfeitures

Title 33 Navigation; Parts 26, 67, 80, 107, 110, 158–162, 164–167, 173–187, 207, 334

- ❑ 26. Bridge-to-Bridge (B2B) Radio

- ❑ 67. Aids to Navigation

- ❑ 80. COLREGS, Demarcation Lines

- ❑ 107.200. Cuba

- ❑ 110. Anchorage Regulations

- ❑ 151. Vessels carrying oil, noxious liquid substances, garbage, municipal, or commercial waster, and ballast water

- ❑ 153. Control of pollution by oil, and hazardous substances, discharge removal

- ❑ 155. Oil, or hazardous material pollution prevention regulations

- ❑ 158. Reception facilities for oil, noxious liquid substances, and garbage

- ❑ 159. Marine sanitation devices

- ❑ 160. Ports, and waterways safety–general

- ❑ 161. Vessel traffic management

- ❑ 162. Inland waterways navigation regulations

- ❑ 164. Navigation safety regulations

- ❑ 165. Regulated navigation areas, and limited access areas

- ❑ 166. Shipping safety fairways

- ❑ 167. Offshore traffic separation schemes

---

[39] See URL link at page 101 for most recent CFR information. Note that this list of: Parts and Sections is very complete, but not absolutely.

[40] Don't be misled by the description. Some sections apply to *recreational* craft. See U.S. Customs page 62.

- ❑ 173. Vessel numbering, and casualty, and accident reporting
- ❑ 174. State numbering, and casualty reporting systems
- ❑ 175. Equipment requirements
- ❑ 177. Correction of especially hazardous conditions
- ❑ 179. Defect notification
- ❑ 181. Manufacturer requirements
- ❑ 183. Boats, and associated equipment
- ❑ 187. Vessel identification system
- ❑ 207. Navigation Regulations (Army Corps of Engineers, inland waterways)
- ❑ 334. Danger Zones

The Navigation parts in Title 33 are mostly included in the excellent reference material in the U.S. Coast Pilots. Each Pilot's chapter № 2, has the Navigation Regulations. Note that parts 26, 67, 80, 110, 160–166, and some others, are enforced by the USCG. Parts 207 and 334: by the Army Corps of Engineers.

Title 40 Environment: Parts 91, 94

- ❑ 91. Gas Engines
- ❑ 94. Diesel Engines

Title 46 Shipping: Parts 7, 24, 25, 67, 69, 159–164

- ❑ 7. Boundary Lines
- ❑ 24. General Provisions
- ❑ 25. Requirements
- ❑ 67. Documentation
- ❑ 69. Measurement of vessels
- ❑ 159–164. Equipment Approvals

Title 46 is especially complex as it is divided into Subchapters.

Subchapter

A; parts 1–9 applies to most vessels.

C; parts 24, 25 contains regulations for un-inspected vessels, which includes recreational, which are exempt if under 19.8 meters if powered, or 700 gross tons or less if sail.

G; parts 67, 69 contains Documentation.

Q; parts 159–164 contains approvals.

COMMERCIAL

All the subject matter in Title 46, Subchapters B, D-F, H-P, R-W: B(10–16), D–F(30–64), H–P(70–158), R–W(165–199), and parts 4, 26, 27, 28, and 68 pertains to commercial vessels only. If someone quotes you something from *any* of the *parts* mentioned in *this paragraph*, then that part does not apply to recreational vessels. Part 4 is casualty reporting for commercial vessels only (recreational vessel reporting comes under Title 33 part 173).

Title 47 Radio: Parts 80 (Subpart X), 97 [41]

- ❏ 80. Maritime Ship
- ❏ 97. Amateur Radio

Title 50 Wildlife: Part 227

- ❏ 227. Threatened Fish & Wildlife [42]

Cuba

U.S. Boats need:

1. USCG permit
2. License from the U.S. Treasury (33 CFR 107.200).

http://www.cubacruising.net/

U.S. Treasury Web Site

http://tinyurl.com/qy8v7 [xl]

This is a readable summary of the U.S. Laws.

http://tinyurl.com/2jtpee [xli]

The USCG permit information can be seen at this link:

http://tinyurl.com/2p2etv [xlii]

U.S. Customs Regulations

See: Title 19, most of Part 4, specifically for Cruising Licenses Section 4.94, see page 10.

Specifically, Sections: 0, 1, 2, 3, 4, 6, 8, 9, 14, 39, 50–52, 60, 61, 65, 66, 94, 95, 98.

- ❏ 0. General definitions
- ❏ 1. Boarding of vessels; cutter, and dock passes
- ❏ 2. Reports of arrival of vessels
- ❏ 3. Vessels required to enter; place of entry
- ❏ 3a. Penalties for violation of vessel reporting, and entry requirements
- ❏ 6. Departure, or unlading before report, or entry
- ❏ 8. Preliminary entry
- ❏ 9. Formal entry
- ❏ 14. Equipment purchases by, and repairs to, American vessels
- ❏ 39. Stores, and equipment of vessels, and crews' effects; unlading, or lading, and retention on board
- ❏ 50. Passenger lists
- ❏ 51. Reporting requirements for individuals arriving by vessel
- ❏ 52. Penalties applicable to individuals

---

[41] See Summary of Part 80 at page 56.

[42] U.S. Coast Pilot 9 contains descriptions for the protected Steller Sea Lion rookery sites. Part 227 is enforced by NOAA.

- ❑ 60. Vessels required to clear
- ❑ 61. Requirements for clearance
- ❑ 65. Verification of nationality, and tonnage
- ❑ 66. Verification of inspection
- ❑ 66a. Illegal discharge of oil, and hazardous substances
- ❑ 66b. Pollution of coastal, and navigable waters
- ❑ 66c. Oil pollution by oceangoing vessels
- ❑ 94. Yacht privileges, and obligations
- ❑ 94a. Large yachts imported for sale
- ❑ 95. Records of entry, and clearance of vessels
- ❑ 98. Navigation Fees

There may be a few items missing from these lists of CFR, but not many.

A general overview of the CFRs related to mariners.

http://tinyurl.com/5fpgjg [xliii]

Notes for Non-U.S. Flag Vessels

The Rules apply to you for:

Radio Transmissions: see Title 47, Parts 80, 97.

The Boundary Lines: see Title 46, Part 7.

Foreign Flag yachts are technically subject to Title 46, Subchapter C, the same as U.S. yachts, see part 24.05-1;[43] Canadian yachts are exempt, see 24.15-5. "C" contains parts 24–28, which you can find explained in *Federal Regulations for Pleasure Craft.*[44]

Most of the Navigation Rules: see Title 33 (above) Parts 26, 158–167, and Casualty reporting in 173, Sec. 51–59.

Especially note the Bridge-to-Bridge Rules if over 20 meters (47CFR80.163, and 33CFR26), in the appendix to the COLREG; also see page 1 for a download web site link.

U.S. Coast Pilots

Each Coast Pilot's first two chapters contain summary information of vital importance to: mariners, including recreational boaters, see page 17.

Chapter 1 contains General Information and is identical in all nine Pilots. Chapter 2 contains the Navigation Regulations and is similar in each Pilot, but has specific navigation details for the area of the Pilot.

Every mariner should be familiar with the contents of these two chapters.

---

[43] Rarely enforced

[44] http://tinyurl.com/dfr8dy

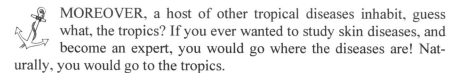

Section 9 – ▷
Medical

Malaria & Yellow Fever

MOREOVER, a host of other tropical diseases inhabit, guess what, the tropics? If you ever wanted to study skin diseases, and become an expert, you would go where the diseases are! Naturally, you would go to the tropics.

[45]

Malaria is not to be taken lightly, and is extremely lethal in some areas. Even if you do not die, you may have recurrences for decades afterwards. Contracting a disease will not only cost you time, and money, but may prevent you from traveling on to your next intended country.

- Do not become paranoid about the danger; but at the same time do not become complacent.

- Successful treatment of malaria requires prompt attention to the symptoms and examination by a doctor. Delay can be fatal.

- Malaria is highly fatal in some areas. The danger is related to which of the four parasitic strains is prevalent in the region.

- Not all victims who survive are cured. You may be infected for life.

- Taking medication in advance is highly recommended, but is not 100% effective.

---

[45] I require medical assistance.

- Not being bitten is the best solution. Wear light *colored* clothing. Use DEET[46] on you, but not your clothing. Sleep under netting.

- Permethrin[47] is an insect **killer and** *repellent*; apply to clothing.

- Avoid known malaria areas, if at all possible. Take precautions appropriate to the risk.

- "Malaria mosquitoes" are out at dusk, and during the night.

- "Dengue mosquitoes" are out during the daytime, around buildings.

- Spread from *infected* mosquitoes to people, and vice versa, round, and round

- Yellow Fever now has a vaccine, see the CDC.[48]

Recommend that you check the CDC web site for the latest information about any area that you are going to visit.

Take precautions to avoid being bitten by insects. They are the most frequent carriers of all tropical diseases. If you spray on DEET, be sure to **rub it out** to guarantee it is spread evenly.

On the Web, search in Google using *mosquito netting* for the search string. *Cabelas* carries DEET, Permethrin, other outdoor equipment, and are reliable suppliers.

http://www.cabelas.com/

Malaria Atlas Project

http://www.map.ox.ac.uk/

A Malaria Vaccine is under development and shows promise. Check for latest information. Even if the vaccine is described as worthwhile, it may not be 100% effective. At the least, continue to use repellent and netting.

---

[46] http://en.wikipedia.org/wiki/DEET

[47] http://en.wikipedia.org/wiki/Permethrin

[48] http://tinyurl.com/2aqnse

US Centers for Disease Control (CDC)

http://wwwn.cdc.gov/travel/

Inspect sub topics under Travel.

Mosquitoes & Tick Protection

Travel Medicine Clinics. Vaccinations

Malaria Risk Map

Outbreaks: Malaria, or Yellow Fever.

Notice: Malaria Outbreak – Bahamas

http://tinyurl.com/2zn4tp

Also, Notices by Country, before you visit.

Regions & Destinations

Beef, Poultry, Meats, Vegetables & Fruits

The authorities are concerned about introduced diseases as well as unwelcome outside species of plants, and animals.

Bilge water contains organisms from other regions. Your refrigerator contains plants and meats from other ecosystems, and these may contain organisms that can cause trouble. Take precautions to prevent spreading such organisms around, even where you are not going to be hassled about them.

Once at sea, pump your bilge when leaving port, and then, while still beyond sight of land, pump it again before making your next landfall. You might even put a little bleach in the bilge water; no more than if you were going to drink it.

Cook up any meats, or plant foods that may not be acceptable to keep upon arrival. Do not try to fool the authorities. Even if you are not caught, it will *get around* and leave a bad impression.

Beef and "Mad Cow Disease" is going to be around for a long time. The root cause of this disease is not cured by cooking, or freezing the beef. If beef is on the banned list, be sure to use it up before making landfall. Here is the wiki article: http://tinyurl.com/39ggeo

Night Vision

- Night vision consists of rods, and cones.

- Rods are 1000 times as sensitive, but only distinguish intensity, not color.

- Cones are only sensitive to color, but only operate from about 15° from straight ahead.

- Your night vision is enhanced by vitamin A, which supports your *Visual Purple*.

- It can take 30 minutes to recover your night vision after even a few seconds of bright light.

Web Site Resources

http://tinyurl.com/o5bf3 [xliv], http://tinyurl.com/2vtpxg [xlv]
http://tinyurl.com/yt4seg [xlvi], http://tinyurl.com/2v7ss7
[xlvii]

Section 10 – Navigation

 ## Buoy Systems A & B

IALA System B is used in the U.S., including Hawaii & Pacific Trust, North, South & Central America, Bermuda, Philippines, Japan, and So. Korea — IALA System A is used **everywhere** else. This includes the South Pacific, Taiwan, and Greenland.

In the **B** System, Red Buoys are kept to the *right* on entering from sea; in the **A** System, it is the opposite.

http://tinyurl.com/yqoo7b [xlviii]

The IALA regulations **do not** specify the numbering system.

In the U.S.: Red Buoys are **Even** numbers and Green, **Odd**. However, Bermuda is part of Region B, and its Red Marks are numbered **Odd**.

Here is a trick to help. When coming from sea, the right hand side day

mark is always TRIANGULAR

The left hand side marks are SQUARE

Regardless of color!

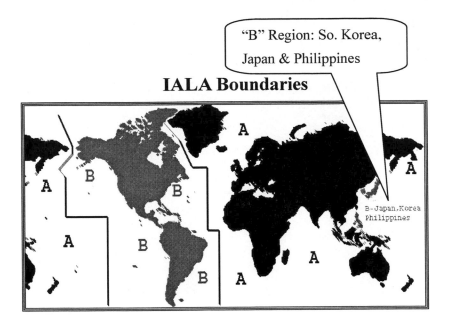

Figure 10 – IALA Region Map

Maps

http://tinyurl.com/27yfnj [xlix]

http://tinyurl.com/282m2v [l]

Atlantic

80 N & between Canada & Greenland to:

55 W & 55 N to 35 W

South to 5 N to 20 W

20 W, south to 65 S.

Pacific

80 N down Dateline to 10 N

East to 120 W

120 W, south to 65 S.

Cardinal Marks

Used outside the U.S., mostly in Region A, especially where **returning from sea** is not obvious, and, a Lateral Buoy or Mark would be ambiguous.

http://tinyurl.com/23m2hf[li]

Figure 11 – Cardinal Marks[49]

The colors are Black & Yellow; this is not apparent from the picture.

The safe water is in the indicated TRUE direction.

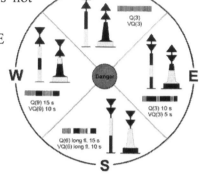

At night cardinal marks flash as follows:

- ☐ North: continuously. ⸻ ⸺ ⸻
- ☐ East: 3 times. — — —
- ☐ South: 6 times,

    plus a long flash. — — — — — — ⸻
- ☐ West: 9 times. — — — — — — — —

Note, that this is similar to a clock face: 3 o'clock for east; 6 o'clock for south, etc.

---

[49] by Reinhard Kraasch

Sailing Directions

Similar to the U.S. Coast Pilots; coverage is worldwide. Contains Navigation Regulation Information; details of obstacles, ports, anchorages, weather, currents, tides, fishing times, and places, see NGA page 93.

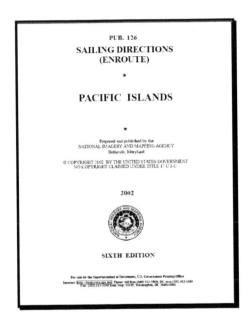

Vessel Traffic Services – VTS

If you approach any of the major ports in the world, most of them have a VTS, which is not the same as a **Traffic Lane**, which the VTS most likely has several.

The edges of the Traffic Lanes are very important, and you need to know exactly where the edges are.

There are places where there are Traffic Lanes, but **no** VTS, such as in the waters north of Japan and east of Russia.

If you do not have detail charts, you will have severe difficulty knowing where the traffic lane edges are.

The World VTS web site has *Plans,* which contain diagrams of the VTS area, and the rough location of the Traffic Lanes.

http://www.worldvtsguide.org/

What you really need is the start and end-points in GPS format, accurate to within 100 feet. This level of detail is difficult, but not impossible to obtain.

I put the start and end-points of the edges in my GPS so I can see the edge of the lane as a line in my GPS on the chart-plotting page. This works even with a handheld GPS such as the Garmin 76 units.

In the U.S., the edges of the lanes are defined in the Coast Pilots, see Chapter(s) 2, Part 167, also in, CFR Title 33 Part 167, see sample for N.Y.:

http://tinyurl.com/37adcm

The Strait of Juan De Fuca Lanes are not listed in Part 167.

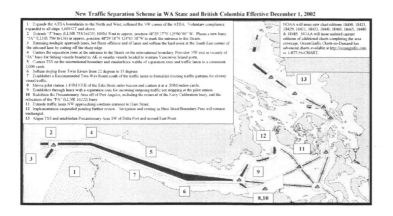

Figure 12 - Traffic Lanes, Strait of Juan De Fuca & BC

Direction Lights

A direction light shows White down the centerline, a Red light over the location where a Red Buoy would be placed, and a Green light over the area that a Green Buoy would be placed.

This means that the Red will be on the starboard side when returning from sea in the IALA System B, and Green in the System A region, and so on.

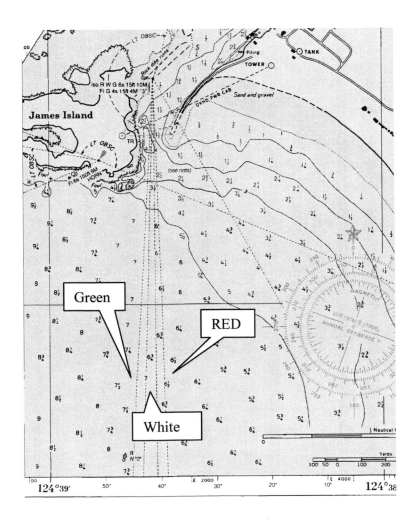

Figure 13 – Chart 18480-2, Quileute River, WA. Entrance

Notice the direction light layout on the chart. The green sector is on the left, white in the middle, red on the right. Note also that the buoy, which is red, is just to the left of the green sector, in this particular case. The buoy has been moved from year to year. Of course, the rocks have not been moved!

See how the white beam sector will carry you safely through the entrance, even though there are rocks only 30 feet on your left, going-in.

At night, it is a wise precaution to verify that the light is aligned correctly. In a safe location, some distance from the light, run back and forth to verify all three sectors are visible, and that the sectors lie where they should be. The edge of each colored sector is only a few feet apart, even at 1,000 feet. You can test this by zigzagging back, and forth, while still in the safe area.

There is always a small chance of the light being damaged, and not reported. If it is damaged in any respect, report it immediately, by radio, to the authorities.

Section 11 – ▷ ▷ Formal Ship's Business

 AN introduction to the formal process that big ships are subjected to, and to which *you* might be! Actually, you do not really want to know about these issues. However, if you are subjected to some obscure procedure, it probably will be one of these.[50]

Documents and Certificates

- Certificate of Documentation
- Crew List
- Ship Radio Station License
- Shipping Articles
- Derat
- Life raft Test & Inspection
- Insurance for Liability for Oil Pollution
- Master Carpenter's Certificate
- Fire Extinguisher Test & Inspection
- Tonnage Tax Receipts

- Bridge Record Card
- International Load Line Certificate
- Cargo Ship Safety Construction Certificate
- Passenger Ship Safety Certificate
- Stability Letter
- Financial Responsibility (Water Pollution)
- International Oil Pollution Prevention Certificate
- Tonnage Certificate
- Deadweight Certificate
- Equipment Certificate
- Freeboard Assignment
- Notice of Preferred Fleet Mortgage
- Grain Loading & Stability Letters
- Register of Cargo Gear

Official Logbook

Deck Log, Bell Book, Medical, Oil Record, Radio, Course Recorder.

50

Merchant Marine Officers Handbook: page 112.

Section 12 – ▷ ▶
Miscellaneous

Single-Handing

AIS

AIS[51] uses: VHF channels 87B and 88B which are in the *International* channel set, rather than the *U.S.* set. If you set up a handheld radio to listen to 87B, turn the squelch and the volume up high, so that only a strong signal will break the squelch; then when a big ship comes near, using AIS, you will be notified of its presence. Done this way you should get warning when the big ship is about 6–10 miles away.

Modern VHF sets have U.S., International, and Canadian modes. To get 87B, or 88B, you have to put the radio in International mode. Check your radio's documentation for instructions. Verify that the set is using the "B" channel by examining the screen. There will be a "B" after the channel number; if it is an "A" you do not have it set up correctly.

Lookout

Keep a careful visual lookout, supplement with radar, and monitoring of the VHF on channels 13, 16, and DSC 70.

Numbering & Documentation

Early Renewal

The ship's Document can be renewed early (CG-1280). Use this to renew when it is convenient to fax the renewal to the document center

---

[51] See page 98

and it might be difficult later to renew before the present document expires. You can renew as often as you need. For instance, if the present document expires in six months but you will not, or might not, be able to send and receive the renewal just before it expires, renew now.

Form 1280 can be obtained from the website below, or use a copy of page: 86.

http://tinyurl.com/2rqg8u [lii]

Fax the form to:

 +1-304-271-2405

Do not send the current document to the Coast Guard, or surrender the original to anyone; it should always be aboard the vessel. If you need "real copies", obtain certified ones from the C.G., see Ordering Copies.

Certified Copies of the ship's Document are available for $4 each; this is much preferable to questionable ones made on your copy machine.

http://tinyurl.com/2wowro [liii]

Vessel Tender Documented?

Documentation of your vessel does **not** cover the vessel's tender or dinghy. These craft fall within the jurisdiction of the motorboat numbering laws of the state of principal use. Contact your state agency that handles the registration or numbering of motorboats, for further information.

http://tinyurl.com/3bu6ed ^{liv}

Boat Name

If covered by the dinghy must be visible some other place on the mother vessel.

Numbered Vessels

A vessel that is numbered by the U.S. Coast Guard (currently all states do their own numbering), and any state that provides for it in their regulations, can allow a tender that is not separately numbered or registered.

At the option of each state:

Where the tender does not have an engine of more than 10 horsepower, and that it is used solely to transport persons from that vessel directly to shore, and *for no other purpose*. This is state dependent, and if you operate with any powered dinghy out of state, or in a foreign country that it would be wise to register and number the dinghy-tender separately.[52]

Where the mother vessel is *Numbered*, and the tender is not being numbered separately, then the number for the tender consists of the numbered vessel's Number to which a space, or dash, has been added as well as the number[53] "1", or "2" in sequence (ex. WA–1234–XX–1)

Documented Vessels

Where the tender is associated with a *Documented* vessel, if the tender has a motor of any kind, or size, then the tender has to be registered separately, no exceptions except lifeboats (tenders are not lifeboats). You can confirm this by consulting a recent copy of Chapman's Piloting & Seamanship.

---

[52] CFR 46, Sec.173.13 Exemptions

[53] See Empire of Bluewater in the Bibliography.

Documentation, State Registration & Insurance

The following issues generally apply to non-U.S. citizens buying a boat in the US.

You can cruise in the U.S. with a state registered boat (not documented), and this is most likely the best, most convenient way. If you take the boat to another country besides the U.S., it is time to think about getting it documented. If the boat is not owned by U.S. citizens, then you cannot get it documented U.S. You may be able to get it documented by your home country, but in some cases you may not be able to do so until the boat arrives back in your home country.

In any event, each change of registration-documentation may affect your ability to obtain insurance. Foreign clearance may be very difficult to do unless the boat is documented somewhere (not just registered). Documentation is easily verifiable, whereas registration is not. The difference in time to do this verification could be on the order of days or weeks. In the meantime, the authorities are entitled to hold you while it is being done.

Do not ever identify your vessel's flag country by flying a flag of a different country; it is a sure way of getting into trouble. In other words, if you change the registration or documentation to another country, do not continue to fly the flag of the previous documentation country. Do not fly the flag of your birth country, your residence country, etc., as identification of where the vessel is documented.

You are vulnerable to being boarded on the High Seas, by any governmental ship of any country, if you are not flying the flag of the country from which your documentation has been issued. This vulnerability also includes registered, not documented vessels, traveling the High Seas. If you are not documented, you may be taken (the boat) into custody while its legitimacy is verified. None of this is very likely to happen, but the way to prevent it is to have your act together and all your papers in order.

- Fly your vessel's flag as identification for the country where it is presently registered-documented. If the vessel's flag country changes, change the flag you fly.

- Expect delays in foreign clearing, if not worse, if the vessel is not documented. If you have to travel with a non-documented vessel, prepare the way in advance of your arrival. Fax your papers to your next destination, and make sure they know you are not documented. Carry a certified Apostille copy of your registration title.

- Getting insurance may be difficult, or impossible for international travel, if the vessel is not documented. Advise your insurance company concerning the steps you are taking to avoid problems with the lack of being a documented vessel.

- Buying a boat in a foreign country can be complicated and frustrating. There are a myriad of tax, duty, insurance, and documentation issues to be dealt with. If you intend to cruise in the country where the boat is being bought, consider chartering it under a bare-boat charter, until you get it where you want to change its registration; this might include taking it all the way home. This assumes that the original contract has a termination sale-clause in it, where you finalize buying it.

- Taking delivery of the boat in a duty free zone, or port, may be one way to simplify the process.

Bare boat charter - wiki

http://tinyurl.com/283amz

USCG Bare Boat Chartering

http://tinyurl.com/2bpxru

A U.S. documented vessel that has any endorsement other than recreational can not be operated by a non-U.S. citizen. If it has a recreational endorsement in addition to other endorsements, then it can be operated under its recreational endorsement, with the provision that the operation must be recreational in nature. The USCG Vessel Documentation Center's, frequently asked questions[54], states that any U.S. documented vessel can be operated as recreational, even if it does not have a recreational endorsement. In any event, operating as a recreational vessel means that the appearance of it being recreational must be maintained, for instance, no commercial fishing gear, no merchandise, or goods, or paying passengers being carried.

---

[54] See VDOC FAQ at page 103

If the boat looks like, or has been used for commercial purposes, and it is engaged in any activity that has the appearance of being commercial in nature, it will get careful scrutiny from the authorities.

Earthquakes

An earthquake that occurs while you are afloat is not liable to be noticeable unless you are in shallow water. John Rains reported that he experienced an earthquake while in Mexico; the boat was underway. The noise was as if the boat had gone aground. There is a small but real possibility of a Tsunami occurring at the same time.

Port Royal, Jamaica was destroyed by an earthquake and subsequent Tsunami that occurred in the late 1600's. The ground, which was sand, liquefied, the buildings literally sank into the sand and the sea washed over the area to a height of 30 feet. The entire process was attributed to "The Wrath of God!" as Port Royal had the reputation as being the most degenerate place on earth! Pirate Captain Henry Morgan's coffin reportedly floated up, out of the sand, and was swept out to sea.

Tsunami

If you are anchored in shallow water, with a Tsunami approaching, your options are limited and require immediate attention. Being anchored is better than being swept into the shore, but not as desirable as being in *deep* water. If you are sure that you can up-anchor, and get to deep water; that is one thing.

But, if you cannot get to deep water, remember that the speed of the water in shallow water as it surges towards shore can easily exceed 20 knots. The average cruiser cannot reach such speeds. And, if attempted to run against the surging water, would be swept back into the shore.

In general you are *safer* inside your boat and anchored, than outside and underway, if in shallow water.

This brings up the definition of Shallow Water. There is no simple number that can be used to determine a safe-water depth. Just take it for granted that deeper is better, that 100 feet should be safe in many cases, but not all.

Grounding

There are two types of grounding, soft, and hard. It is not within the scope of this book to describe the actions to be taken to get off, but the legal issues are. I have reports that a hard grounding in Mexico that cannot be gotten off within some period of time, 24-48 hours, will result in the boat being confiscated by the authorities. In addition, you may be held responsible for damage to coral reefs, spilled fuel, as well as the cost of any salvage effort needed to get the boat free.

Remember, if this becomes a salvage operation; do not proceed until you have a signed salvage agreement, preferably one where you do not pay unless you get a "cure". There is such an agreement on page 172.

U.S. laws related to groundings, wrecks, and abandonment are in 33USC407-9, 14, and 15. Finding the Mexican or other country versions of similar laws is difficult, but reading the U.S. versions will give you a reasonable idea of what is involved.

Appendix

☎International Telephone Dialing

DIALING across the international phone system can be tricky. Be sure to test your dialing access to a test number using the same dialing access that would be needed for any of the emergency numbers that I have included.

It is assumed that any phone number you call that came from this book is being dialed from a satellite phone, or from outside the country where the number is located. The dialing codes have the format where the leading "+" is the access to international dialing. The digit(s) that immediately follow are those of the **Country Code**, followed by the so-called **Local Number**.

For instance, +1-202-123-1234 is a number for the U.S. country code "1"; the area code is 202, and the local number is 123-1234; such a number would in Washington DC.

The international dialing prefix is generally "011", or "001", and depends upon where you are dialing from. In the case of an Iridium satellite phone, the "+" button can be pressed, and held until the "+" is visible in the screen. Then the country code and local number can be entered, this simplifies the procedure.

The example above would be 011-1-202-123-1234, from the Iridium, if not using the special "+" key.

Here is a URL that provides online lookup for dialing instructions, by country.

http://www.countrycallingcodes.com/

or

http://tinyurl.com/2oufa

For instance, dialing from UK to U.S., the international access code is: "00", whereas, from the U.S. to UK, it is "011"; then, followed by the country code and number.

Here are the WIKI country code information pages with many links to more detail:

http://tinyurl.com/joxfw [lv]

You may see numbers provided by others who did not understand the International Access Code, and they may have confused the situation by adding what they thought was the access code, when in fact depending upon the called from country the code may be one of the ones I mentioned above, but it might be something else entirely.

For instance, "Transiting the Panama Canal" by David Wilson gave a phone number of:

011-507-223-4146

The actual number is

+507-223-4146

He assumed that the access code was 011 plus the number, but that is not always correct. By the way, the "4146" is the same as the frequency number for a SSB channel just above 4.125 MHz. The access code would be whatever it is; in the country you are calling from, such as 00, 011, etc.

More confusion can come about. Once I was given a Mexican number similar to this:

044-624-999-1234

However, the number can only be dialed this way from a Mexican phone, most likely a landline. In, order to dial from the U.S., Iridium, etc., you need the country code 52, and of course the access code "+".

+52-624-999-1234

Or, 011-52-xxx-xxx-xxxx

However, there is one more wrinkle. The actual phone I was calling was a cell phone, and such a phone requires an additional "1" after the 52 country code, such as:

+52-1-624-999-1234

You will run into many similar combinations. I do not have a complete set of rules to help stop this confusion. However, this web site should provide the answers:

http://www.kropla.com/dialcode.htm

or

http://tinyurl.com/mm5nb

North American Dialing Code One (1)

American Samoa	Anguilla
Antigua	Bahamas
Barbados	Bermuda
Canada	Cayman Islands
Dominica	Dominican Republic
Grenada	Guam
Jamaica	Montserrat
Northern Mariana Islands	Puerto Rico
St. Kitts and Nevis	St. Lucia
St. Vincent and the Grenadines	Trinidad and Tobago
Turks and Caicos Islands	Virgin Islands, British
Virgin Islands, All 50 U.S. States	U.S. Military Islands, Pacific Basin

Islands in the Pacific associated with the U.S. Military, such as Wake Island, have phone numbers with a country code of One (1). The phone service is Iridium Satellite based using a special access gateway located in Hawaii (this information included in case of an emergency).

U.S. Documentation Renewal

RENEWING ENDORSEMENTS ON A CERTIFICATE OF DOCUMENTATION

Vessel owners are required to renew the endorsement(s) on Certificates of Documentation each year. Failure to renew the endorsement(s) may result in the vessel being removed from documentation. Operation of a vessel with expired endorsements may result in a civil penalty.

If the vessel has been lost, sold, abandoned, destroyed, or *placed under state numbering*; the vessel owner must notify the National Vessel Documentation Center in writing. If the Certificate of Documentation is available, it must be surrendered. If any of the information shown on the Certificate of Documentation, other than the address of the owner, has changed, please contact The National Vessel Documentation Center for advice on how to proceed. The toll free telephone number is 1-800-799-8362.

The endorsement(s) may be renewed by completing the substitute form CG-1280 that is on the following page. NOTE: it may be renewed at **any time** before expiration and will have an expiration of just over twelve months from the date of the new issuance.

Be sure to write the Name and Document Number on the form, sign and date it, and then fax it.

The Certification may be sent by facsimile (fax) mail to the National Vessel Documentation Center at +1-304-271-2405. Although facsimile submissions are preferred, the Certification may be mailed to the National Vessel Documentation Center, 792 T J Jackson Drive, Falling Waters, WV 25419. You can make a **copy** of this page, fill in the form, and fax it to the U.S. Vessel Documentation Center. Or, send the signed form to: nvdc.pdf.filing@uscg.mil (the form should be in PDF format, sent as an attachment). Details at: http://www.uscg.mil/hq/cg5/nvdc/nvdcpdf.asp

Substitute CG-1280

RENEWAL CERTIFICATION

I CERTIFY THAT THE RECITATIONS ONCERNING VESSEL NAME, TONNAGE, DIMENSIONS, PROPULSION, OWNERSHIP, RESTRICTIONS, ENTITLEMENTS, and EMPLOYMENT CONTAINED IN THE CERTIFICATE OF DOCUMENTATION ISSUED TO THE VESSELS NAMED BELOW HAS NOT BEEN LOST, MUTILATED, or WRONGFULLY WITHHELD.

NAME(S), *and OFFICIAL NUMBER(S)* OF VESSELS COVERED BY THIS CERTIFICATION: (May be listed on an attachment if necessary)

OWNER'S ADDRESS (IF CHANGED FROM ADDRESS SHOWN ON CERTIFICATE OF DOCUMENTATION)

_____

Authorized Signature

_____   _____

Capacity of Person   Signing Date

Cruising License Reciprocity

Title 19 CFR Section 4.94

(b) A cruising license may be issued to a yacht of a foreign country only if it has been made to appear to the satisfaction of the Secretary of the Treasury that yachts of the United States are allowed to arrive at, and depart from ports in such foreign country, and to cruise in the waters of such ports without entering, or clearing at the customhouse thereof, and without the payment of any charges for entering, or clearing, dues, duty per ton, tonnage, taxes, or charges for cruising licenses. It has been made to appear to the satisfaction of the secretary of the Treasury that yachts of the United States are granted such privileges in the following countries:

See page 12 for the list of countries.

Note: the U.S. does not charge for a Cruising License, and reciprocating countries should not be either. If they do, a complaint should be directed to the U.S. State Department.

Federally Licensed Pilot

Here is the legal basis, for obeying the regulations, where a Federally Licensed Pilot is required by state or federal laws.

Title 46, Sec. 15.812 Pilots

(2) An individual holding a valid license issued by the Coast Guard as master, or mate, employed aboard a vessel within the restrictions of his, or her license, may serve as pilot on a vessel of not more than 1,600 gross tons propelled by machinery, described in paragraphs (a)(1), and (a)(3) of this section, provided he, or she:

(i) Is at least 21 years old;

(ii) Complies with the currency of knowledge provisions of Sec.10.713 of this chapter; and

(iii) Has completed a minimum of four round trips over the route to be traversed while in the wheelhouse as watchstander, or observer. At least one of the round trips must be made during the hours of darkness if the route is to be traversed during darkness.

Sec. 10.713 requires a round trip within the last 60 months, or familiarization by consulting charts, and other written material.

Internet Resources

If a URL link no longer works, try removing the text after the web site definition so that you will be taken to the main page, since the specific page may have been deleted, or renamed.

Note: some of the web links failed to work properly, I have inserted a tinyurl link that generally works, and have left the original in case you have to enter the string by hand. The longer web links have been placed in the End Notes section, page 174.

FCC Ship's License Help

http://www.shiplicense.com/

List of Customs Web Sites

A general list of 67 countries

http://www.aduanaargentina.com/listado_en.php?seccion=24

By Country

Argentina

http://www.aduanaargentina.com/listado_en.php?seccion=30

Australia

http://www.customs.gov.au/site/page.cfm?u=4260

http://www.customs.gov.au/site/page.cfm?u=4791

or

http://tinyurl.com/2xz42j

Bermuda	.customs.gov.bm
Chile	.aduana.cl
Canada	.cbsa.gc.ca
China	.customs.gov.cn
Cuba	.aduana.cu
Hong Kong	.customs.gov.hk
Indonesia	.beacukai.go.id
Japan	.customs.go.jp
Maldives	.customs.gov.mv
New Zealand	.customs.govt.nz

New Guinea

.customs.gov.pg/yachts.html

S. Korea	.customs.go.kr
Singapore	.customs.gov.sg
S. Africa	.sars.gov.za
Thailand	.customs go.th
Turkey	gumruk.gov.tr
UK	customs.hmrc.gov.uk

Foreign Country's Embassies in US

http://www.state.gov/s/cpr/rls/dpl/32122.htm

or

http://tinyurl.com/3cs6gc

Embassies by Country

http://www.embassyworld.com/

or

http://tinyurl.com/32xp78

💀 Office of Naval Intelligence Piracy Reports

http://pollux.nss.nima.mil/onit/onit_j_main.html

or

http://tinyurl.com/2lwyf6

💀 ICC Commercial Commerce Piracy Page

http://www.icc-ccs.org/prc/piracyreport.php

or

http://tinyurl.com/9sztl

U.S. Internet Sources

United States International Trade Commission

http://www.usitc.gov/tata/hts/bychapter/index.htm

or

http://tinyurl.com/2eb9am

Flags

http://www.boatsafe.com/nautialknowhow/flags.htm

or

http://www.flagline.com/gp01A

Embassies, Consuls

http://usembassy.state.gov/

or

http://tinyurl.com/heqpn

State Department Notes, by Country

http://www.state.gov/r/pa/ei/bgn/

or

http://tinyurl.com/4srq5

Pleasure Boats

http://www.cbp.gov/xp/cgov/travel/pleasure_boats/

or

http://tinyurl.com/2wzpq6

http://www.drugstory.org/drug_traffic/smuggling.asp

or

http://tinyurl.com/32fblp

💀 Reporting Suspicious Activity

U.S. Customs

 +1-800-BE-ALERT

Security, or actual smuggling.

Customs Districts

Schedule D

http://hotdocs.usitc.gov/docs/tata/hts/bychapter/0800statannx.pdf

or

http://tinyurl.com/yutp6w

Establishing Residency

http://hubpages.com/hub/state-residency

or

http://tinyurl.com/2pocwe

U.S. Inland Cruising

Great Loop

http://en.wikipedia.org/wiki/Great_loop

or

http://tinyurl.com/35n9qr

New York Canals

http://www.nyscanals.gov/exvac/boating/index.html

European Cruising

Canal Regulations

http://www.canals.com/

http://www.bargingineurope.com/licensing.htm

or

http://tinyurl.com/3dnnuy

Size information

http://www.canals.com/size.htm

or

http://tinyurl.com/39y5lm

RYA European Waterways Regulations

The CEVNI Rules Explained

http://tinyurl.com/2nyorg [lvi]

There is also a Waterways Manual; a cruising guide.

Adlard Coles Inland Waterways.

Foreign Cruising
Vol. 1: Atlantic Coast of Europe & Baltic Sea
Vol. 2: Mediterranean, and the Black Sea

International Certificate of Competency

http://www.rya.org.uk/KnowledgeBase/boatingabroad/icc/

or

http://tinyurl.com/2qude8

Seasickness

http://curingseasickness.com

Smuggling In the Old Days

Britain

http://www.smuggling.co.uk/buybook.html

or

http://tinyurl.com/3d2g74

Web Pages of Country Info

http://www.noonsite.com/Countries

U.S. Vessel Search

http://tinyurl.com/3dowxb

USCG Regulations

Marine Safety Manual

* Volume 1 – Administration, and Management
* Volume 2 – Materiel Inspection
* Volume 3 – Marine Personnel
* Volume 4 – Technical
* Volume 5 – Investigations
* Volume 6 – Ports, and Waterways Activities
* Volume 9 – Environmental Protection

http://www.uscg.mil/hq/g%2Dm/nmc/pubs/msm/

or

http://tinyurl.com/355gq6

Light Lists

USCG

http://www.navcen.uscg.gov/pubs/LightLists/LightLists.htm

or

http://tinyurl.com/yvcbw6

Notices to Mariners

USCG – Local Notices

http://www.navcen.uscg.gov/lnm/

or

http://tinyurl.com/3ykwu7

NGA – Notices

http://tinyurl.com/3xk8jb [lvii]

British Admiralty

http://www.ukho.gov.uk/amd/noticeToMariners.asp

or

http://tinyurl.com/2wadbp

Australia

http://www.hydro.gov.au/n2m/notices.htm

or

http://tinyurl.com/33lzgx

New Zealand

http://www.hydro.linz.govt.nz/ntm/index.asp

or

http://tinyurl.com/2uxnt9

Various other Governments and local jurisdictions: too extensive to list here. Search Google, "notice to mariners"; also, enter in a country, or local jurisdiction name.

Wiki – Notice to Mariners

http://en.wikipedia.org/wiki/Notice_to_Mariners

or

http://tinyurl.com/2wxcc3

NGA Publications

http://tinyurl.com/lh2nr

Mariners Handbook (NP100), British Admiralty, Extracts from Navigation Regulations.

http://tinyurl.com/yonyft

Official Logbook, PDF

USCG C.G.–706

http://www.uscg.mil/hq/gm/marpers/logbook.pdf

or

http://tinyurl.com/2hshn6

Articles of Agreement

CG–705

http://tinyurl.com/24mlln

U.S. Code Documents (USC)

http://www.gpoaccess.gov/uscode/index.html

or

http://tinyurl.com/2ezshe

There is a relation between USC documents and CFR documents. However, they are not the same. If you have a reference that is in a USC section, then you will have to search in that part of the GPO.

For instance, go to the links provided above to find "19 USC 1401k", enter in the *search window*, "19USC1401" (leave out the quotes).

- CFR – U.S. Code of Federal Regulations, non-static laws. Executive Branch.
- USC – U.S. Code, laws of the U.S., mostly static. Congressional Branch.

http://uscode.house.gov/download/download.shtml

Current General Country Information

U.S. Department of State Consular Sheets, by Country

http://travel.state.gov/travel/cis_pa_tw/cis/cis_1765.html

or

http://tinyurl.com/4ow7g

Shanghaiing

http://wapedia.mobi/en/Shanghai_(verb)

or

http://tinyurl.com/ywn65q

No Discharge Zones

http://www.epa.gov/owow/oceans/regulatory/vessel_sewage/vsdnozone.html

or

http://tinyurl.com/2f69rn

Yachtsmen Visiting Canada

http://www.tc.gc.ca/marinesafety/debs/obs/quick/quick_visitor.htm

Power of Attorney

You need a power of attorney form to provide the authority for someone to take charge of the boat in case the Captain of Record is incapacitated. If the Captain dies, you need a Durable Power of Attorney.

http://en.wikipedia.org/wiki/Power_of_attorney

A Limited Durable Power of Attorney

To whom it may concern:

I, xxxxxx, owner of the vessel xxxxx, USA (or whatever) registration number, (include the HIN if available), do authorize that in the event of my death, incapacitation due to illness, or injury, or absence that the following herein named individual, (xxxxx name), be empowered with all the authority of Captain of Record for any purpose that may be necessary for the vessel. Specifically to: operate or sail said vessel, make arrangements for trans-shipment, storage, or to hire another Captain to perform the same.

The individual authorized above, shall be authorized to sign legal documents necessary for the vessel's operation, or to carry out this power of attorney.

Signed this xxxx day of xxxx 200x

Signature

Witnessed by:

Xxxxx, xxxx

Notarized by

Xxxxxx

You will also need a power of attorney for someone to handle some of your affairs, back home.

Warning: the Power of Attorney may not be recognized if the person who authorized it, is dead. Such an enduring power is called a Durable Power of Attorney.

Technical Contacts

FLIR

Their Export expert is Melissa Wilkinson.

☎ +1-805-690-7176, The ECCN № for the Mariner model is 6A003, section B

Definitions

Admiralty Law

http://en.wikipedia.org/wiki/Admiralty_law

Admiralty Law comes to us from maritime traditions formulated by Roman and Byzantine compacts, and later by the Hanseatic League, a trade guild whose influence extended from the Baltic to the North Sea during the 13–17th centuries.

When Eleanoire of Aquitaine, mother of Richard the Lionheart returned from The Crusades with her first husband, the French King; she introduced Admiralty Law into her realm, and later into England when she was regent for her son. [55]

Admiralty Law is not based on English Common Law but stems from the Corpus Juris Civilis of the Emperor Justinian. Admiralty Courts are civil courts with a judge but no jury.

Captain of Record

The individual listed as such, on the ship's Clearance Form, issued at the last port.

Clearance Form

This is a document that officially makes leaving the country legal; known as a *Zarpe* in some countries. You must have the original to hand to the authorities at the next port. Make sure that the document can be verified as being an original. Be sure the ink from the signature

---

[55] See the film: "The Lion in Winter"

and stamp penetrates to the opposite side of the document, as this indicates an original not a copy from a copying machine.

COLREG
International Regulations for the Prevention of Collisions, see page 1.

Law of the Sea (LOTS)
http://www.globelaw.com/LawSea/ls82_1.htm

or

http://tinyurl.com/2s9981

Foreign Country
The land territory and the adjacent territorial sea[56].

Government Printing Office (GPO)
The United States government's printing office.

Innocent Passage, Right of

See LOTS, Part 2, Sec. 3, page 148. As of 2003 there were 157 signatories, and 143 ratifications of the Law of the Sea.

For instance, for U.S. and Canadian boaters, there are times where you cross back and forth over the boundary. So long as you do not tie up, anchor, **or** come into physical contact with a vessel that has yet to clear U.S. or Canadian customs, you are not in violation of any law or regulation. Innocent Passage has obligations as well as a Right; no threat to the nearby country, use of, or practicing with arms, spreading propaganda, etc.

Innocent Passage allows one to *pass through* Canadian or other foreign waters.

Territorial Sea
No more than 12 nautical miles.

---

[56] Territorial, Contiguous & EEZ Claims see page 153.

See table page 153 for TS and CZ.

Contiguous Zone

Generally, no more than 24 miles, within which a state can exert, limited control for the purpose of preventing, or punishing:

infringement of its customs, fiscal, immigration, or sanitary laws, and regulations within its territory, or territorial sea.

The U.S. zone is 24 miles.

Tables by Country, Territorial Sea, Contiguous Zone & EEZ

http://en.wikipedia.org/wiki/Territorial_waters

or

http://tinyurl.com/2pxp3d

See also tables page 153.

Hindering Innocent Passage

See LOTS. Sec. 3, Articles 22, 23, 24, 25, 26, see page 148.

Innocent Passage

A concept in Admiralty Law, also defined in LOTS, which allows a vessel to pass through the territorial waters of another state subject to certain restrictions.

The U.S. Dept. of Defense defines innocent passage as:

The right of all ships to engage in continuous, and expeditious surface passage through the territorial sea, and Archipelagic waters of foreign coastal states in a manner not prejudicial to its peace, good, order, or security.

Passage includes stopping, and anchoring, but only if incidental to, ordinary navigation, or necessary by force majeure, or distress, or for the purpose of rendering assistance to persons, ships, or aircraft in danger, or distress.

There is some difference between the UN definitions and the U.S. Dept. of Defense, see page 148.

Anchoring is a touchy subject. In some areas, anchoring may be necessary due to fishing gear, and other obstacles.

Going ashore or having a contagious disease would constitute a breaking of the rules. In other words, do not abuse the right, do not make excuses that are not supportable.

If you are going to anchor you had best be well up on the attitude of the local authorities, and the provisions of the Law of the Sea, see page 148, for details.

Other Definitions

AIS

Automatic Identification System transmits on VHF channels 87B, 88B: position, speed, and other information about nearby vessels.

http://www.navcen.uscg.gov/enav/ais/default.htm

or

http://tinyurl.com/3yhfg9

Apostille

Double certification is required by some countries, where the issuing country or state certifies the authenticity of the document signer.

http://www.state.gov/m/a/auth/

or

http://tinyurl.com/3aw6ce

A good explanation can be found at this site.

http://www.apostille.us/

Carnet

An International customs document used to simplify customs procedures for the temporary importation of various types of goods. A kind of "Merchandise Passport", see page 43.

Certified Copy

Copies made and certified by the agency issuing the original document; also copies certified by a Notary Public.

CFR

United States Code of Federal Regulations: executive branch regulations and orders. See U.S. Code Documents, page 93.

DSC – Digital Selective Calling

DSC SC-101 is *NOT* equivalent to Class D, and has been withdrawn from handheld radio use. Class A uses a *second* receiver to listen on channel 70.

EEZ – Exclusive Economic Zone

Generally out to 200 miles.

http://en.wikipedia.org/wiki/Exclusive_Economic_Zone

or

http://tinyurl.com/2whnb5

NLR

Mass Market products are eligible for export with NLR (No License Required) to any end user (including government end users) in all countries except the seven (7) embargoed countries: Cuba, Iran, Iraq, Libya, North Korea, Sudan, and Syria. Mass Market products are eligible for de minimis treatment.

http://www.esri.com/legal/export/export-definitions.html

or

http://tinyurl.com/2m3y3e

Flag Country

Is the country to which a vessel is registered.

Foreign Built Vessel

A vessel for which the ship's document specifies a shipyard outside the U.S.

If the vessel's keel, or hull, was laid in a U.S. shipyard then it is entitled to be classified as U.S. built; be sure your ship's Document and paperwork reflects this fact. If there is any question about the vessel's build country be sure to hang onto the Builder's Certificate C.G.–1261.

ITU

International Telecommunications Union is the agency that settles the rules for international radio communications issues.

http://www.itu.int/net/home/index.aspx

or

http://tinyurl.com/322osx

MMSI Number

Maritime Mobile Service Identity Number

Issued by the FCC, or your country's radio licensing bureau; installed in your transmitters. Used by the DSC system, see page 56.

http://www.navcen.uscg.gov/MARCOMMS/GMDSS/mmsi.htm

or

http://tinyurl.com/2trgop

Be sure to check the ITU database to be sure your number, and identification information are correct, and your EPIRB is correctly associated with the MMSI:

ITU MMSI search

http://www.itu.int/cgi-bin/htsh/mars/ship_search.sh#start

http://tinyurl.com/2purm3

Mutiny

Is the taking control from the Master of the Vessel by more than one person.

No Cure, No Pay

A concept in salvage law, that there is no point in paying for salvage work unless the benefit is appropriate to the expense; the salvage must be successful for there to be any payment.

Proof of Duty

If you cannot find, or have a copy, or original of the duty paid for a *foreign* built vessel, here are some steps that you can take that will *help*.

Have the boat examined by a Customs officer and have them certify a Customs Form 4457, Certificate of Registration for Personal Effects

Taken Abroad. Fill out the form with the boat's information; this will prove that the boat is not being brought into the U.S. for the first time.

An alternate tactic is to have a Certified copy of the "Abstract of Title".

Any proof that you have that the boat was previously in the U.S. should be of some help; receipts such as: fuel, repairs, moorage, a U.S. Customs Clearance form (see page 26), or Clearance Number. You record Clearance Numbers in your logbook, right?

Sail Vessel

A sail vessel is a vessel with no auxiliary machinery on board. If the vessel has machinery it is not a sail vessel.[57]

State of Principle Use

Underway, moored, anchored, in the water, or tied to a dock; constitutes the place of principle use. On a trailer or ashore does not constitute "use". A dinghy carried on deck, in davits but not in the water, is unlikely to be considered "use". Reciprocity is guaranteed by the Motor Boat Act of 1971 for a minimum 60 days.

U.S. Code of Federal Regulations (CFR)

Most recent U.S. CFR's

http://www.access.gpo.gov/nara/cfr/cfr-table-search.html#page1

or

http://tinyurl.com/x9q7

CFR 33 = Navigation & Navigable Waters (generally recreational regulations).

CFR 46 = Shipping (generally commercial with some recreational regulations).

See U.S. Laws of Interest to Recreational Yachtsmen, page 60.

---

[57] Title 46: Subpart 24.05-1. See table footnote 13.

FSBA 1971

Federal Safety Boating Act of 1971, and its predecessors in 1956 and 1941, in: CFR Title 33: Part 173.

USC

United States Code: laws passed by the U.S. Congress. It uses the same Title Number and Naming scheme as the CFR, but not for the subparts.

VAT – Value Added Tax

Prevalent in Europe: the EU.

Avoiding VAT http://tinyurl.com/yr6tpr

VAT on vessels http://tinyurl.com/2ef5uh

Voyage Data Recorder

A type of: *Flight Recorder* for large commercial vessels.

Zarpe

A clearance form: for a foreign clearance or perhaps an internal one used to go from port to port within a country such as Mexico.

Boating Regulations by U.S. STATE [58]

http://www.boatus.com/onlinecourse/states/

or

http://tinyurl.com/3e2afy

Boating Regulations: see Chapman's.

No details by state, but very comprehensive.

USCG National Vessel Documentation Center

http://tinyurl.com/2kyzem [lviii]

---

[58] Incomplete

VDOC FAQ

http://www.uscg.mil/hq/gm/vdoc/faq.htm

or

http://tinyurl.com/2jjwx5

Ordering Copies

Abstract of Title online, or certified copies of the ship's Document:

https://vcart.velocitypayment.com/uscg/

or

http://tinyurl.com/3afpow

Merchant Marine Officers Handbook

Fifth Edition pages 459–61. In the ship's business chapter are the following interesting notations. Keep in mind that these do **not** apply directly to pleasure craft.

- The ship's document is to be deposited with the U.S. Consul at any port where there is one, until the ship departs. Most major ports have a U.S. Consul.

- Not all ports issue a formal Clearance Document. The ship's agent is responsible for providing the ship with a letter attesting to this fact.

- If the local Customs people place seals on cabinets or cabins, they must not be broken until the Pilot has been dropped off and the ship is headed for sea.

There are major fines for breaking these rules.

World Wide

Cruising Information

http://asianyachting.com/default.htm

http://www.noonsite.com/

Embassy Web Sites

— A —

AFGHANISTAN

http://www.embassyofafghanistan.org/

ALGERIA

http://www.algeriaus.org/

ANGOLA

http://www.angola.org/

ARMENIA

http://www.armeniaemb.org/

AUSTRALIA

http://www.usa.embassy.gov.au/

AUSTRIA

http://www.austria.org

AZERBAIJAN

http://www.azembassy.us/

— B —

BANGLADESH

http://www.bangladoot.org/

BAHRAIN

http://www.bahrainembassy.org/

BELARUS

http://www.belarusembassy.org/

BELGIUM

http://www.diplobel.us/

BELIZE

http://www.embassyofbelize.org/

BENIN

http://www.beninembassy.us/

BOLIVIA

http://www.boliviausa.org/

BOSNIA, and HERZEGO-VINA

http://www.bhembassy.org/

BOTSWANA

http://www.botswanaembassy.org/

BRAZIL

http://www.brasilemb.org/cultural/washington_events.shtml

BRUNEI

http://www.bruneiembassy.org/

BULGARIA

http://www.bulgariaembassy.org/

BURKINA

http://www.burkinaembassyusa.org/

BURUNDI

http://www.burundiembassyusa.org/

— C —

CAMBODIA

http://www.embassyofcambodia.org/

CAMEROON

http://www.ambacamusa.org/

CANADA

http://geo.international.gc.ca/canam/washington/menuen.asp

CHILE

http://www.chileusa.org/

CHINA

http://www.chinaembassy.org/eng/

COLOMBIA

http://www.colombiaemb.org/opencms/opencms/

COSTA RICA

http://www.costaricaembassy.org/

CROATIA

http://www.croatiaemb.org

CYPRUS

http://www.cyprusembassy.net/home/

CZECH REPUBLIC

http://www.mzv.cz/wwwo/?zu=washington

— D —

DENMARK

http://www.ambwashington.um.dk/en

DOMINICAN REPUBLIC

http://www.domrep.org/

— E —

ECUADOR

http://www.ecuador.org

EGYPT

http://www.egyptembassy.net/

EL SALVADOR

http://www.elsalvador.org/

ESTONIA

http://www.estemb.org/

ETHIOPIA

http://www.ethiopianembassy.org/index.shtml

— F —

FIJI

http://www.fijiembassydc.com/

FINLAND

http://www.finland.org/en/

FRANCE

http://www.ambafranceus.org/

— G —

GAMBIA

http://www.gambiaembassy.us/

GEORGIA

http://www.georgiaemb.org/

GERMANY

http://www.germany.info/relaunch/index.html

GHANA

http://www.ghanaembassy.org/

GREAT BRITAIN, UNITED KINGDOM OF

http://www.britainusa.com/

GREECE

http://www.greekembassy.org/Embassy/content/en/Root.aspx

GRENADA

http://www.grenadaembassyusa.org/

GUATEMALA

http://www.guatemalaembassy.org/main.php

GUINEA

http://guineaembassy.com/

GUYANA

http://www.guyana.org/govt/foreign_missions.html

— H —

HAITI

http://www.haiti.org/

HOLY SEE

http://www.holyseemission.org/

HONDURAS

http://www.hondurasemb.org/

HUNGARY

http://www.huembwas.org/

— I —

ICELAND

http://www.iceland.org/us

INDIA

http://www.indianembassy.org/newsite/default.asp

INDONESIA

http://www.embassyofindonesia.org/

IRAN

www.daftar.org

IRAQ

http://www.iraqiembassy.org/

IRELAND

http://www.irelandemb.org/

ISRAEL

http://www.israelemb.org/

ITALY

http://www.ambwashingtondc.esteri.it/ambasciata_washington

— J —

JAMAICA

http://www.jamaicanconsulatechicago.org/

JAPAN

http://www.embjapan.org/

JORDAN

http://www.jordanembassyus.org/new/index.shtml

— K —

KAZAKHSTAN

http://www.kazakhemb
us.com/

KENYA

http://www.kenyaemba
ssy.com/

KOREA

http://www.koreaemba
ssyusa.org/

KYRGYZ REPUBLIC

http://www.kyrgyzemba
ssy.org/

— L —

LAOS

http://www.laoembassy
.com/

LATVIA

http://www.latviausa.or
g/

LEBANON

http://www.lebanonem
bassyus.org/

LESOTHO

http://www.lesothoemb
usa.gov.ls/

LIBERIA

http://www.embassyofli
beria.org/

LIECHTENSTEIN

http://www.liechtenstei
n.li/

LITHUANIA

http://www.ltembassyu
s.org/

LUXEMBOURG

http://www.luxembourg
usa.org/

— M —

MACEDONIA

http://www.macedonia
nembassy.org/

MALI

http://www.maliembass
y.us/

MARSHALL ISLANDS,
REPUBLIC OF

http://www.rmiembassy
us.org/

MEXICO

http://portal.sre.gob.mx
/usa/

MICRONESIA

http://www.fsmembass
ydc.org/

MOLDOVA

http://www.embassyrm
.org/

MONGOLIA

http://www.mongoliane
mbassy.us/default.php

MOZAMBIQUE

http://www.embamoc-
usa.org/

MYANMAR

http://www.mewashingt
ondc.com/

— N —

NAMIBIA

http://www.namibiane
mbassyusa.org/

NEPAL

http://www.nepalemba
ssyusa.org/

NETHERLANDS

http://www.netherlande
mbassy.org/homepage
.asp

NEW ZEALAND

http://www.nzembassy.
com/home.cfm?c=31&l
=86&CFID=428854&C
FTOKEN=39748729

NIGER

http://www.nigerembas
syusa.org/

NIGERIA

http://www.nigeriaemb
assyusa.org/

NORWAY

http://www.norway.org/
Embassy/embassy.htm

— P —

PALAU

http://www.palauemba
ssy.com/

PANAMA

http://www.embassyofp
anama.org/

PAPUA NEW GUINEA

http://www.pngembass
y.org/

PERU

http://www.peruvianem
bassy.us/

PHILIPPINES

http://www.philippinee
mbassyusa.org/

POLAND

http://www.polandemb
assy.org/

PORTUGAL

http://www.portugal.org
/index.shtml

— Q —

QATAR

http://www.qatarembas
sy.net/

— R —

ROMANIA

http://www.roembus.org/

RUSSIA

http://www.russianembassy.org/

— S —

ST. VINCENT, and THE GRENADINES

http://www.embsvg.com/

SAUDI ARABIA

http://www.saudiembassy.net/

SIERRA LEONE

http://www.embassyofsierraleone.org/

SERBIA

http://www.yuembusa.org/

SINGAPORE

http://www.mfa.gov.sg/washington/

SLOVAK

http://www.slovakembassyus.org/

SOUTH AFRICA

http://www.saembassy.org

SPAIN

http://www.mae.es/Embajadas/Washington/en/Home/

SRI LANKA

http://www.slembassyusa.org/

SURINAME

http://www.surinameembassy.org/

SWEDEN

http://www.swedenabroad.se/pages/start_6989.asp

SWITZERLAND

http://www.swissemb.org

— T —

TAJIKISTAN

http://www.tjus.org/

TANZANIA

http://www.tanzaniaembassyus.org/

THAILAND

http://www.thaiembdc.org/index.htm

TUNISIA

http://tunisiaembassy.org/

TURKEY

http://www.turkishembassy.org/

TURKMENISTAN

http://www.turkmenistanembassy.org/

— U —

UGANDA

http://www.ugandaembassy.com/

UNITED ARAB EMIRATES

http://uaeembassy.org/

UKRAINE

http://www.mfa.gov.ua/usa/en/news/top.htm

URUGUAY

http://www.uruwashi.org/

UZBEKISTAN

http://www.uzbekistan.org/

— V —

VENEZUELA

http://www.embavenezus.org/

VIETNAM

http://www.vietnamembassyusa.org/

— Y —

YEMEN

http://www.yemenembassy.org/

— Z —

ZAMBIA

http://www.zambiaembassy.org/

— EUROPEAN UNION —

http://www.eurunion.org

Table of Night Vision Properties

Rods	Cones
Primarily for night vision	Primarily for day vision
Highly sensitive to light; sensitive to scattered light (more pigment than cones)	Less than 1/10th of the rods' light sensitivity; sensitive only to direct light
Slower response to light; rods need to be exposed to light over time	Quicker response to light; can respond more rapidly to changes in light intensity, and color.
Provides black/white/gray vision, with more emphasis on detecting motion	Provides color vision, with more emphasis on detecting fine details
One type of photosensitive pigment (monochromatic stimulus)	Three types of photosensitive pigment in humans (trichromatic stimulus)
22 times as numerous as cones in the retina	
Low spatial resolution with higher noise	High spatial resolution with lower noise
None in the fovea (center)	Mostly in the fovea (center)
Loss causes degrees of night blindness	Loss constitutes legal blindness
Stacks of membrane-enclosed disks are unattached to the cell membrane	Disks are attached to the outer membrane

U.S. State Tax Issues

Definition of Real Versus Personal Property

Real Property is generally real estate, whereas, boats, planes, and RV's are Personal Property.

Property Taxes

Personal Property Taxes on boats are local taxes; which means county and city. Boats may, or may not, be exempt from Personal Property Taxes, by state, county, or city. See page 124, and for more detail information, also:

http://tinyurl.com/2w4tjd

The table of Property Tax States, where the table indicates no tax, only applies to *recreational* boats. For instance, Washington State taxes commercial boats. Where boats are not taxed, it is generally due to the notion that since they do not produce income, they are exempt as in Texas.

There may be a few places where there is a property tax administered by some other government agency; the possibility cannot be absolutely excluded.

If you are a transient, being present in a marina on tax day, which is most likely January 1st, may allow you to become entangled unnecessarily in the local tax system. In which case, the safest bet is to be moored in a state that does NOT allow property tax on boats, or if they do, not in a county, or city that does so.

The tax due in such cases most likely consists of two parts, the county one, and the city one. The city part is most likely a fraction of the county part. The valuation placed on the boat does not necessarily equal the market value. This last is another variable that is hard to pin down.

An example would be Edenton Marina, NC, where you have to pay the annual city and county property tax, $56 county and $29 city per $10,000 valuation, i.e. for $100,000 property, you pay $850.

You cannot rely on verbal or even written opinions from state tax employees, or, what is written here. In some states not even the opinions of local expert tax attorneys.

Maryland is the poster child for a state where you cannot rely upon any opinion except maybe the Judge who tries your case, maybe not even the Judge.

The tables provided here cannot be relied upon, as they contain unknown errors. Use only as a rough guide to assist you in doing your own research.

There are numerous exemptions to the Sales/Use and Property Tax Laws, some to your benefit and some not. There are complex exemptions for used boats, sometimes private sales.

None of this may apply to, or should be relied upon at all, if you are a resident of the state. In point of fact, this entire book is not intended as guidance for a resident of their own state.

Do not respond to demands for information. Once you do, they then have added incentive to keep hounding you, and you have created an implied obligation to continue to reply. Providing false information is a felony in many states, which is an added incentive not to reply.

If you become involved in the property tax system, you may also be hit for sales/use tax.

Some state tax employees have been reported to deliberately mislead, in order to enhance tax revenue, or fail to provide forms. In some cases the forms are now on the Internet.

There are basically three types of boat owners; those passing through, those trying to identify a suitable place to retire[59], or to moor somewhere distant from their place of residence. The material supplied here is intended for those passing through.

Property Taxes at city owned marinas. In some cases the tax is passed on as a separate bill, be sure to ask. Private marinas generally have the taxes built into the marina fee.

---

[59] http://www.retirementliving.com/RLtaxes.html

Under the exemptions topic is the issue of when the tax kicks in, by date, or minimum time. In some cases, the tax is owed for vessels on site on January 1, or whatever. In other cases, it is dependent on how many days you have been in the state.

There are probably exceptions to these generalizations. The only safe bet is to verify the situation in the target locale

Visit my web site page: http://tinyurl.com/39lac6

Instructions for locating current state/county/city tax rates.

Latest Sales Tax Rates, single page table

http://www.taxadmin.org/FTA/rate/sales.html

or

http://tinyurl.com/pezxf

Detail Information about State Taxes

http://www.bankrate.com/brm/news/news_taxes_home.asp

or

http://tinyurl.com/yrv8bl

This web site above is an excellent source of information, very comprehensive.

Picking A State

Occasionally, someone asks the question about picking the ideal state to register a boat, or get state validation decals if the boat is documented.

This not an answer, but it will help you to make a choice.

1. The most desirable states are those without Sales/Use taxes, or on private sales.

2. States without property taxes on boats.

3. States that actually issue decals to documented boats.

If you eliminate all of the tax states and include only the ones that issue decals, there are only four states.

DC, NH, OR, RI

❏ District of Columbia charges $15–60 per year.

- Rhode Island charges $30–600, approximately $2–12 per foot per year.

- Oregon charges $3 per foot for a two-year decal.

- Arizona is reported to not have sales tax on private sales.

There may be some exceptions but in general, this is accurate information. There are states that fit № 1, and № 2 above, but do not issue decals. It may be possible to get one of them to issue a decal if you are a resident. It will not hurt to ask.

By the way, Florida charges $1 to $2 per foot per year for its registration tax, which is really only useful to transients.

The Ultimate Guide to Offshore Tax Havens, $20–30

http://tinyurl.com/2tfnpl

Definitions for State Table

Consecutive

For instance, if a documented vessel from another state is brought into North Carolina for over 90 *consecutive* days, the decal must be purchased from North Carolina.

Registration w/Validation Decal

If the vessel is Documented; Yes, means the state requires a decal to be purchased and displayed after the reciprocity period expires. In some cases the state requires a decal *immediately*, if you do not have a current, in-force-decal from some state, see Reciprocity Issues, page 45.

Reciprocity at State Boundaries

Oregon and Washington share a common boundary at the Columbia River. Boaters from either state have reciprocity from the other state, while boating on the river. Other states most likely, have, similar arrangements, ask around for details.

Table of State Abbreviations & Boating Tax Administrators[60]

Be sure to check the update phone numbers in the table on page 119.

STATE NAME	ABREEVIATION	CONTACT. BLA – BOATING LAW ADMINISTRATOR	☎ PHONE [61]
Alabama	AL	Bill Garner, BLA, Marpol Dir.	(334) 242-3673, #4
Alaska	AK	Jeff Johnson, BLA, Dept. of Natural Resources	(907)463-2297
Arkansas	AR	Mike Wilson, BLA, Boating Safety Section	(602)942-3000
Arizona	AZ	Mark Weise, BLA, Game & Fish Dept.	(501)223-6378
California	CA	Don Waltz, Chief of Boating Facilities Division	(916)657-8013
Colorado	CO	Rick Storm, BLA, Div. of Parks & Outdoor Rec.	(303)791-1954
Connecticut	CT	Eleanor Mariani, BLA, DEP: Boating Div.	(860)566-1556
Delaware	DE	Chief Jim Graybeal, BLA; Div. of Fish & Wildlife	(302)739-3498
District of Columbia	DC	Lt. Alfred Durham, Metro Police Dept., Harbor Ptrl Sec.	(202)727-4582
Florida	FL	Sandra Porter, FFWCC, Div. of Admin. Services	(850)488-4676
Georgia	GA	Lt. Col. Terry West, DNR, Wildlife Resources Div.	(770)414-3337

---

[60] The Phone Numbers are not to the Contact for the BLA in some cases, but to the Registration Administrator.

[61] See Alternate Phone number table

STATE NAME	ABREEVIATION	CONTACT. BLA – BOATING LAW ADMINISTRATOR	☎ PHONE [61]
Hawaii	HI	Mason Young, Boating Law Administrator, DLNR, Div. of Btg & Ocn. Rec.	(808)587-1970
Idaho	ID	Doug Strong, BLA; Dept. of Parks & Rec, Boating Program	(208)334-4180 x279
Illinois	IL	Greg Hunter, BLA; DNR, Office of Law Enforcement	(217)782-2138
Indiana	IN	Sam Purvis, BLA; DNR, Law Enforcement Div.	(317)233-5096
Iowa	IA	Randy Edwards, BLA; DNR, Fish & Wildlife Div.	(515)281-6579
Kansas	KS	Theri Swayne, BLA; KS Wildlife & Parks	(316)672-5911 x127
Kentucky	KY	Maj. Charles Browning, Dept. of Fish & Wildlife	(502)564-3074
Louisiana	LA	Lt. Col Charles Clark, Dept. of Wldlf & Fisheries	(504)765-2898
Massachusetts	MA	John Maxson, Dept. of Fishcrics, Wildlife & Enviro. Law Enforcement	(207)287-5209
Maryland	MD	Col. Doug DeLeaver, DNR, Natr'l Res. Police	(410)260-3220
Maine	ME	Bill Swan, Dir. of Lic. & Reg., Dept. of Inlnd Fshrs & Wldlf	(617)727-3900
Michigan	MI	Sgt. Henry Miazga, BLA; DNR, Law Enforcement Div.	(517)322-1460
Minnesota	MN	Kim Elverum, BLA; DNR, Boat & Water Sfty. Coordinator	(612)296-2316
Missouri	MO	Col. Jerry Adams BLA; Dept. of Publ. Safety, MO St. Water Patrol.	(601)432-2068

STATE NAME	ABREEVIATION	CONTACT. BLA – BOATING LAW ADMINISTRATOR	☎ PHONE [61]
Mississippi.	MS	Maj. Kenny Neely, BLA; Dept. of Wildlife, Fisheries & Parks, Law Enforcement Div	(314)751-4509
Montana	MY	John Ramsey, BLA; MT Fish, Wildlife & Parks, Law Enforcement Div.	(406)846-6000
Nebraska	NB	Herb Angell, BLA; NE Game & Parks Cmsn, Outdoor Ed. Div.	(402)471-0641
Nevada	NV	Fred Messman, BLA; Div. of Wildlife, Law Enforcement Div.	(775)688-1511
New Hampshire	NH	David T. Barrett, BLA; NH Dept. of Safety, Marine Patrol Div.	(603)271-2333
New Jersey	NJ	Walter Schwatka, BLA; NJ State Police, Marine Services Unit	(609)292-6500
New Mexico	NM	Jerome Madrid, BLA, Enrgy, Mnrls & Natr'l Res, Btg Sfty Sec.	(505)827-0612
New York	NY	Brian Kempf, BLA; Director, Bureau Marine & Rec. Vehicles	(518)474-0445
North Carolina	NC	Capt. Mike Bogdanowicz NC Wildlife Resources - Enforcement	(919)662-4373
North Dakota	ND	Nancy Boldt, BLA; Boat, and Water Safety Coordinator	(701)328-6300
Ohio	OH	Ken Alvey, BLA; DNR, Div. of Wtrcrft	(877)4-BOATERM
Oklahoma	OK	Lt. Bob Sanders, BLA; Dept. of Public Safety, Lake Patrol Div.	(405)521-3221

STATE NAME	ABREEVIATION	CONTACT. BLA – BOATING LAW ADMINISTRATOR	☎ PHONE [61]
Oregon	OR	Paul Donheffner, BLA;, or State Marine Board	(503)373-1405 x254
Pennsylvania	PA	John Simmons, BLA; PA Fish & Boat Cmsn, Bureau of Btg. & Ed.	(717)657-4551
Puerto Rico	PR	Ms. Marisa Gonzalez, BLA; Dept. of Enviro & Natr'l Res, Ofc of Cmsnr of Navigation	
Rhode Island	RI	Steven Hall, BLA; Dept. of Enviro. Mgmt.	(401)222-6647
South Carolina	SC	Maj. Alvin Taylor, BLA; Tony Bates, Comptroller, DNR	(803)762-5034
South Dakota	SD	Bill Shattuck, BLA; Dept. Game, Fish & Parks, Div. of Wildlife	(605)773-3541
Tennessee	TN	Ed Carter, BLA; TN Wildlife Resource Agcy, Boating Div.	(615)781-6618
Texas	TX	Dennis Johnston, BLA, Parks & Wldlf Dept., Law Enf. Div.	(800)262-8755
Utah	UT	Ted Woolley, Boating Coordinator, Div. of Parks & Rec.	(801)297-750
Vermont	VT	Alan Buck, BLA; VT State Police, Marine Div.	(802)828-2000
Virginia	VA	Charles Sledd, BLA; Dept. of Game & Inland Fisheries	(804)367-1000
Virgin Islands	VI	Lucia Roberts Francis, BLA; Dept. of Plng & Natr'l Res., Div. of Enviro Enf.	
Washington	WA	James Horan, BLA; Jim Eychaner, Intragcy Cmte for Otdr Rec.	(360)902-3770,#5

STATE NAME	ABREEVIATION	CONTACT. BLA – BOATING LAW ADMINISTRATOR	☎ PHONE [61]
Wisconsin	WI	John Lacenski, BLA; DNR, Div. of Law Enfrcmnt	(304)558-5351
West Virginia	WV	Lt. Col. Bill Daniel, BLA; DNR, Law Enforcement Section	(608)266-2141
Wyoming	WY	Russ Pollard, WY Game & Fish Dept.	(307)777-4683

Table of Boating Law Administrators

http://myboatclub.com/StateAdmin1.html

Alternate Numbers

This is a table of notes confirming the phone numbers, on page 122, for the various states.

NG = Number not good, in table in book, and perhaps no new number
OK = Number is good.

B = Was Busy

? = Unknown, needs research.

Secondary contacts: where this is a number, it is either a replacement or a secondary contact.

These numbers thought to be good, but not confirmed. And, are included as you may be where it is difficult to find an alternate number.

State	☎ Secondary Contact	☎ Alternate Numbers
AL	OK	
AK	907-465-4361	
AR	?	501-223-6399
AZ	OK	602-989-3383
CA	916-657-6893	916-445-6281
CO	OK	
CT	?	860-434-8638
DE	302-739-9916	
D.C.	OK	
FL	850-617-2000	850-488-5600 x162
GA	706-557-3596	800-366-2661
HI	OK	
ID	208-514-2458	
IL	NG	217-782-6431
IN	OK	

State	☎ Secondary Contact	☎ Alternate Numbers
IA	OK	
KS	NG	785-296-2281
KY	800-858-1549	
LA	NG	225-765-2800
MA	NG	671-727-8589
MD	OK	
ME	207-287-8000	207-624-6555
MI	?	517-335-3414
MN	OK	
MO	NG	573-751-3333
MS	601-432-2400	
MT	OK	
NE	402-471-5462	
NV	OK	
NH	OK	
NJ	?	609-882-2000 x6164
NM	NG	505-827-7173
NY	OK	
NC	919-707-0007	919-371-7191 x251
ND	OK	
OH	NG	614-265-6480
OK	?	405-425-2143
OR	FAX	503-378-2617
PA	NG	717-657-4538
PR		787-242-2340
RI	OK	
SC	B	
SD	OK	
TN	OK	
TX	OK	
VI		809-776-8600
UT	NG	801-538-7341

State	☎ Secondary Contact	☎ Alternate Numbers
VT	????	802-878-7111
VA	OK	
VI		
WA	?	
WI	B	608-266-0859
WV	OK	
WY	OK	

State by State

Registration Offices

Phone Numbers, Reciprocity, Decals[62]

State	Reciprocity Days	Consecutive	Registration w/ Validation Decal
AL	90	**	Yes, if used for pleasure
AK	90		No
AR	90		No
AZ	90		No
CA	120		No
CO	60		No
CT	60		Yes
DE	60	**	No
D.C.	180		Yes
FL	90		Yes
GA	60	**	Yes
HI	90		No
ID	60	**	No
IL	60		Yes
IN	60	**	Yes

State	Reciprocity Days	Consecutive	Registration w/ Validation Decal
IA	60		Yes
KS	60		No
KY	60	**	No
LA	90		No
MA	60		No
MD	90		Yes
ME	60	**	No
MI	60		Yes
MN	90	**	No
MO	60		No
MS	60	**	Yes
MT	90	**	No
NE	60	**	No
NV	90		No
NH	30	**	Yes
NJ	180		Yes
NM	Unlimited [63]		Yes
NY	90		Yes
NC	90		NO, but can
ND	180[64]		No

---

[62] See Definitions: page 45

[63] Not required if not permanent resident

State	Reciprocity Days	Consecutive	Registration w/ Validation Decal
OH	60	**	Yes
OK	60		Yes
OR	60		Yes
PA	60		Get valid decal, pay fee every 2 yrs.
PR			
RI	90		Yes
SC	60	**	No
SD	90		No
TN	60	**	Yes
TX	90	**	Yes
UT	14		Yes
VT	30[65]		Yes
WA	60–180[66]	**	No
WV	60	**	No, but can

State	Reciprocity Days	Consecutive	Registration w/ Validation Decal
VI			
WI	60	**	Yes
WY	90	**	No

Use Taxes:
http://tinyurl.com/2dw7pk

Sales Taxes:
http://tinyurl.com/35alra

State of Maryland has increased their reciprocity to 90 days from 30 days. Be warned that MD has a reputation for being pretty ugly about their tax system. Even attorneys that practice there have a hard time giving accurate advice.

Alaska, do not register if documented unless staying. This may apply even to Numbered boats, at least in practice, as they may take pity on you if you stay-over the winter.

[64] Required if primary use

[65] With valid sticker 30-90; register after 90

[66] 60 days, then Apply 2x for 60 permit, total 180; if corporate owned: 60 days only.

Table of State Sales & Property Taxes for Boats

State	Sales Tax	Property Tax, Boats
AL	2%	No
AK	None. Some boroughs with tax	No (State)
AR	4.625%	Yes
AZ	8.1%	No
CA	7.25%	Yes, local
CO	3%	No
CT	6%	No. [67]
DE	No sales	No
D.C.	None	No
FL	6–7.5%	No
GA	3.5% + local	Yes (county)
HI	None	Yes
ID	5%	No
IL	7%	No
IN	5%	No. [68]
IA	5%	No
KS	4.9%	Yes
KY	6%	No
LA	8%	No
MA	5%	No

State	Sales Tax	Property Tax, Boats
MD	5%	No. Excise Tax, one time.
ME	6%	Yes
MI	6%	No
MN	6.5% + 0.5% (in some cities)	No
MO	4.225%	Yes
MS	7%	Yes
MT	No	Yes
NE	5–6%	None
NV	6.5% + local	Yes/ No[69]
NH	No	No
NJ	6%	No[70]
NM	5%	No
NY	4% + local	No
NC	3%, up to $1,500	Yes. 25 – 180/$10,000
ND	5% + local	No
OH	5% + local	No
OK	3.25%	No
OR	No sales	No
PA	6%	No
PR	6.6% local	No
RI	No sales tax on boats	No. Except Westerly

[67] Higher registration fee charged in lieu of taxes.

[68] Excise tax collected each yr based on new value of boat. Each year tax is lowered 10% down to 50% of, original tax

[69] Boat property tax included in boat registration fee

[70] Recreational boat fee based on value of boat

State	Sales Tax	Property Tax, Boats
SC	6% up to $300	Yes. [71]
SD	3% + local	No
TN	8.75%	No
TX	6.25	No
VI	No sales tax on boats	No
UT	4.75% + local (1–2%)	Yes
VT	5%	No
VA	5%	Yes. Not all Local Jurisdictions
WA	7–8.6%	No, Recreational
WI	5% + local	No
WV	6%	Yes
WY	4% + local	No

Table of State Fuel Taxes for Boats & Refunds

State	Type	Fuel Tax Cents	Time Mon	Re-fund?
AL				
A K	G	8	12	3 [72]

State	Type	Fuel Tax Cents	Time Mon	Re-fund?
AR				
AZ				
CA				?
CO				
CT [73]	D,G	25	? [74]	100 %
DE				?
D.				
FL				
G A				
HI				
ID				
IL				
IN				
IA				
KS				
K				
LA				
M	D.G	21	? [75]	100
M D				
M				
MI				
M N				
M	D.G	17	12 [76]	100
M				

[73] Useless, as a use tax will be applied

[74] By May 31st for last year

[75] Useless, as a use tax will be applied

[76] Within 12 months or April 15th, whichever is later

[71] $180/$10,000 approximately

[72] If bought at gas station.

State	Type	Fuel Tax Cents	Time Mon	Re-fund?
M				
NE	D,G	?	36	100
N V				
N				
NJ				
N				
N				
NC	G	24	36[77]	18
N				
O				
O				
OR				
PA				
PR				
RI				
SC				
SD				
TN				
TX	D,G	20	12	100
VI				
UT				
VT				

State	Type	Fuel Tax Cents	Time Mon	Re-fund?
VA	D,G	16-17	12	100%
WA	D	23	1,3, 12	12
WI				
W				
W	D	14	3,12	13

Web sites:

Alaska
http://www.americanboating.org/
fueltax.asp#Alaska

http://www.tax.state.ak.us/forms.
asp

Connecticut
http://www.americanboating.org/
fueltax.asp#Connecticut

http://www.ct.gov/drs/lib/drs/fill
able_forms/2006forms/au-
724fill.pdf

Massachusetts
http://www.americanboating.org/
fueltax.asp#Massachusetts

Missouri
http://www.americanboating.org/
fueltax.asp#Missouri

http://www.dor.mo.gov/tax/busin
ess/fuel/forms/

Nebraska

[77] Prefer within 12 months.

http://www.americanboating.org/
fueltax.asp#Nebraska

http://www.revenue.state.ne.us/f
uels/mfforms.htm

North Carolina

http://www.americanboating.org/
fueltax.asp#NorthCarolina

http://www.dor.state.nc.us/downl
oads/motor.html

Texas

http://www.americanboating.org/
fueltax.asp#Texas

http://www.window.state.tx.us/ta
xinfo/taxforms/06-forms.html

Virginia

http://www.americanboating.org/
fueltax.asp#Virginia

http://www.dmv.state.va.us/web
doc/forms/index.asp

Washington

http://www.americanboating.org/
fueltax.asp#Washington

Wyoming

http://www.americanboating.org/
fueltax.asp#Wyoming

http://www.dot.state.wy.us/Defa
ult.jsp?sCode=bizfq

Coastal States w/Property Tax

State	Property Tax Averages: By State per $1,000 of value	Tax per $100,000
RI [78]	16.72	$1672
ME	13.03	$1303
VI	8.91	$891
GA	8.55	$855
NC	7.63	$763
CA	7.20	$720
MS	6.18	$618
SC	5.49	$549
HI	3.08	$308

Explanation

The Property Tax numbers are averages for the entire state (2000). Are intended for Real Estate (Property), and are provided only as a rough guide as to the likely tax on a Recreational boat in that state. The property tax is especially hard to swallow as it is generally a once a year tax, whereas sales, and use taxes are one time; also excise taxes.

Property Tax States

AK, CA, GA, HI, IN, KS, ME, MO, MS, MT, NV, NC, SC, RI, VA, WV

By Area

AK, CA, HI

ME, VA, WV, GA, MS, NC, SC, RI

IN, KS, MO, MT, NV

By the way, Florida charges $1 to $2 per foot per year for its registration tax, which is really only useful to transients.

New Hampshire has no Sales/Use, or Property Taxes on boats, and *does* issue a decal to documented vessels. However, NH issues the registrations not at the state level. The cost is hard to determine, as it quite variable.

Delaware is an interesting situation. It is common knowledge that many boats are documented, or may be registered in DE, as it has no property or sales tax on boats. However, it does not issue a registration decal to documented boats. Therefore, if you document the boat in DE you will not have the precious decal to fend off the Florida authorities with. I predict that it will not be long before DE does something about this.

Property Tax Exemption

Personal property used as a place of residence, possibly your boat, may be eligible for an exemption to the property tax.

[78] Town of Westerly only

Highest Sales Tax

Then by highest Property Taxes

State	Sales	Property Tax
TN	8.75%	No
WA	7–8.6%	No
AZ	8.1%	No
LA	8%	No
FL	6–7.5%	No
CA	7.25%	Yes, local
MS	7%	Yes
IL	7%	No
MN	6.5% +	No
UT .	4.75% + local (1–2%)	Yes
PR	6.6% local	No
NV	6.5% + local	Yes/ No[79]
TX	6.25%	No
ME	6%	Yes
WV	6%	Yes
CT	6%	No. Higher reg. fee charged in lieu of taxes.
KY	6%	No
MI	6%	No
NJ	6%	Rec. boat. fee based on value of boat
PA	6%	No
NE	4.5–6%	None
VA	5%	Yes, Not all locales

---

[79] Boat property tax included in boat registration fee

State	Sales	Property Tax
ND	5% +	No
OH	5% +	No
ID	5%	No
IN	5%	No. [80]
IA	5%	No
MA	5%	No
MD	5%	No. Excise Tax
VT	5%	No
WI	5% +	No
NM	5%	No
KS	4.9%	Yes
AR	4.625%	Yes
MO	4.225%	Yes
WY	4% +	No
NY	4% +	No
GA	3.5% +	Yes (county)
OK	3.25%	No
CO	3%	No
SD	3% +	No
NC	3%, up to $1,500	Yes. 25 – 180/$10,000[81]
SC	6% up to $300	Yes[82] $180/$10,000 approx.
AL	2%	No
HI	None	Yes
MT	No sales	Yes
RI	No sales tax on	No (except Westerly)
VI	No sales	No

[80] Excise tax collected. Each year based on new value of boat. Each year tax is lowered 10% down to 50% of, orig. tax

[81] http://tinyurl.com/3axl9o

[82] http://tinyurl.com/35oayo

State	Sales	Property Tax
AK	None. Some boroughs w/tax	No (State)
DE	No sales	No
DC	None	No
NH	No sales	No
OR	No sales	No

Property & Sales Tax

Lowest to Highest

	Property Tax on Boats	Boat Sales Tax Rate	Plus Local Tax
AK		0%	
DC		0%	
DE		0%	
NH		0%	
OR		0%	
VI		0%	
AL		2%	
CO		3%	
SD		3%	X
OK		3.250%	
NY		4%	X
WY		4%	X
IA		5%	
ID		5%	
ND		5%	X
NM		5%	
OH		5%	X
VT		5%	
WI		5%	X
CT		6%	
KY		6%	
MA		6%	
MI		6%	
NJ		6%	
PA		6%	
TX		6.25%	

	Property Tax on Boats	Boat Sales Tax Rate	Plus Local Tax
MN		6.5%	X
PR		6.6%	X
IL		7%	
LA		8%	
AZ		8.1% [83]	
TN		8.75%	
NE		4.5-6%	
FL		6-7.5%	
WA		7-8.6%	
HI	X	0%	
MT	X	0%	
RI	X	0%	
GA	X	3.5%	X
MS	X	4.225%	
AR	X	4.625%	
UT	X	4.75%	X
KS	X	4.9%	
IN	X	5%	
MD	X	5%	
ME	X	5%	
VA	X	5%	
WV	X	6%	
NV	X	6.5%	X
MO	X	7%	
CA	X	7.25%	
NC	X	3%, up to $1500	
SC	X	6% up to $300	

---

[83] Arizona does not tax private boat sales. There may be exemptions in other states. Check for current regulations.

The Politics of Property Taxes on Boats

Boat costs go up faster than housing.

Boats generally depreciate, homes generally the opposite.

Boat values are harder to determine, due to custom building, and lack of similar sales to use as guidelines.

The bigger and more expensive the boat: the more incentive to move the boat where it will not be taxed. High property taxes drive boats away.

Legally avoiding the tax is easy enough, that the gain in taxes is often many times less than the loss of general business that accrues from the boat's presence.

Connecticut dropped its property tax on boats in 1981, and replaced it with a simple excise tax, collected at registration time, which is much less costly to administer.

Transients

If you come from a state with no, or low sales/use you are vulnerable in that you can be hit with sales/use tax if you become involved with the property tax system. Since you have not paid a sales/use tax, you could be charged for the difference if you come from a low tax state.

You might not even be liable for property tax, but you could come to the attention of the authorities, and receive an assessment for sales/use tax. If you come from a high sales/use tax state then you cannot be hit with any tax if your original tax was as high, or higher, than the tax in the present jurisdiction. This assumes that you have proof of payment!

The property tax is a sticky problem as you could possibly receive tax bills from two different states for the same tax year. This is very unlikely, but just demonstrates how irrational all this can get.

By the way, the taxman has several lines of attack. There is where the boat is actually moored or used, and, there is where the title is *mailed to*, or where the owner is *located*, or where the *Home Port* is listed, or where you own *property*, and, there may be others. Any of these can create the appearance of jurisdiction, or state of residence, or state of principle use. If you think the legal flypaper is not sticky; well, good luck.

Maps of Coastal U.S. Customs Districts

U.S. West Coast

Washington

Oregon

No. Calif.

So. Calif.

Figure 14 – Washington – California

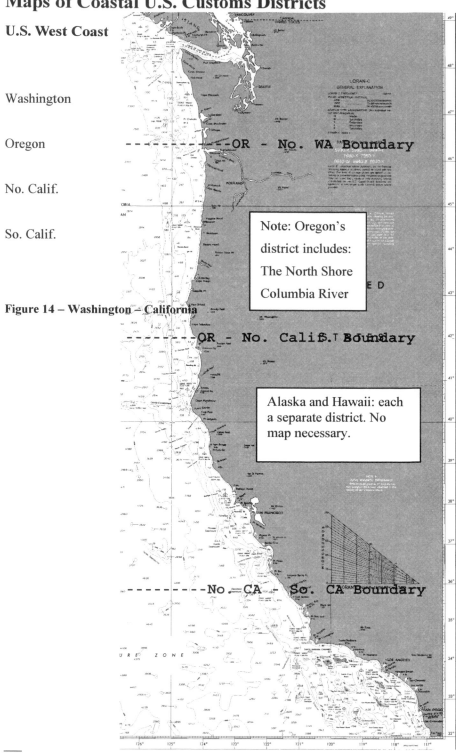

OR - No. WA Boundary

Note: Oregon's
district includes:
The North Shore
Columbia River

OR - No. Calif. Boundary

Alaska and Hawaii: each
a separate district. No
map necessary.

No. CA - So. CA Boundary

Canada – North Carolina

Maine, New Hampshire
Vermont
Massachusetts, Connecticut
Rhode Island
New York, NJ, DE, PA
New Jersey
Pennsylvania
Maryland
DC, Alexandria VA
Virginia, W. Virginia
North Carolina

Figure 15 – Maine – North Carolina

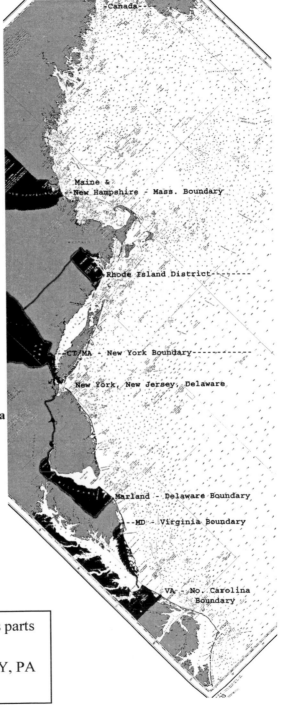

NY has 4 districts, includes parts of NJ.

DE includes parts of NJ, NY, PA

No detail map available

North Carolina – Florida

Figure 16 – North Carolina – Florida

North Carolina
South Carolina
Georgia
Florida

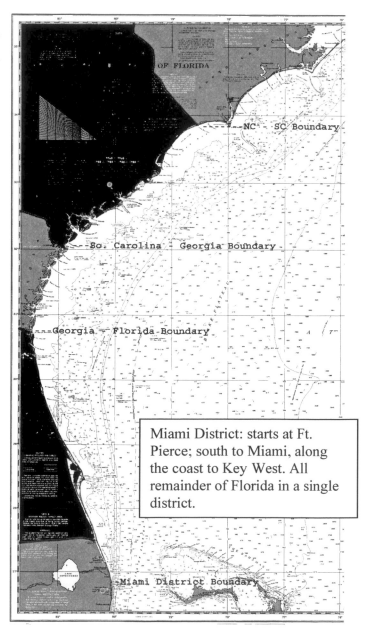

Miami District: starts at Ft. Pierce; south to Miami, along the coast to Key West. All remainder of Florida in a single district.

Brownsville, TX – Georgia

Texas

Louisiana

Mississippi, Alabama

Florida, Miami District

Figure 17 – Gulf Coast States

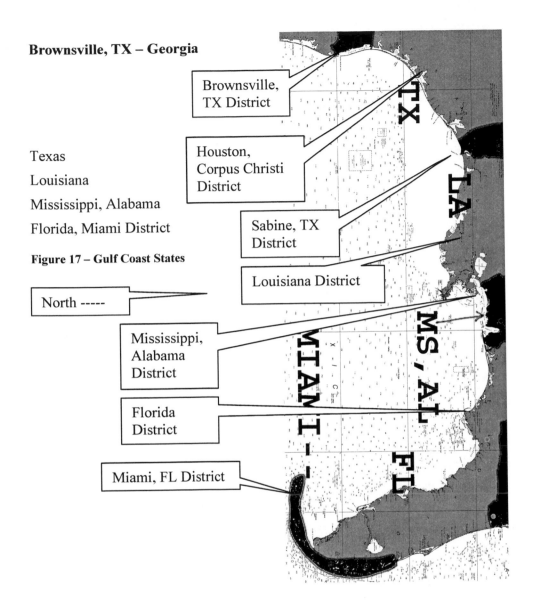

Brownsville, TX District

Houston, Corpus Christi District

Sabine, TX District

Louisiana District

North -----

Mississippi, Alabama District

Florida District

Miami, FL District

Summary of U.S. Customs Districts & Ports

Port District	Includes
Los Angeles, CA	San Diego – Port San Luis. Los Vegas, NV.
San Francisco, CA	All area. Eureka, Reno NV
OR	Coast, all Columbia River including WA + Boise ID.
No. Washington	Coast, All North.
MT	Some ID
AK	All
HI	All
ME, NH	All
VT	All
MA, CT	All
RI	All
NY	4 districts
NY,NJ,PA,DE	Parts
NJ, PA	Parts
MD	All
DC	+ Alexandria VA
VA, VW	Except Alex.
NC	All
SC	All
GA	All
FL	2 districts
AL, MS	All AL.
LA, AR, TN	All, some MS
MN	Minneapolis, St. Paul
MN	Rest, 3 districts
MO	All + KS

MI, WI	All
OH	Also W. KY

Detail Table of U.S. Customs Districts & Ports

CODE #	Port Name
0101	PORTLAND, ME
0102	BANGOR, ME
0102	BREWER, ME
0103	CUTLER, ME
0103	EASTPORT, ME
0103	LUBEC, ME
0104	JACKMAN, ME
0105	VANCEBORO, ME
0106	HOULTON, ME
0107	FORT FAIRFIELD, ME
0108	VAN BUREN, ME
0109	MADAWASKA, ME
0110	FORT KENT, ME
0111	BATH, ME
0112	BAR HARBOR, ME
0115	CALAIS, ME
0115	ROBBINSTON, ME
0118	LIMESTONE, ME
0121	ROCKLAND, ME
0122	JONESPORT, ME
0127	BRIDGEWATER, ME
0131	PORTSMOUTH, NH
0132	BELFAST, ME
0132	BUCKSPORT, ME
0132	SANDY POINT, ME
0132	WINTERPORT, ME
0152	SEARSPORT, ME
0181	LEBANON MUNICIPAL AIRPORT, NH

CODE #	Port Name
0201	ST. ALBANS, VT
0203	RICHFORD, VT
0206	BEECHER FALLS, VT
0207	BURLINGTON, VT
0209	DERBY LINE, VT
0211	NORTON, VT
0212	ALBURG, VT
0212	HIGHGATE SPRINGS/ALBURG, VT
0401	BOSTON, MA
0401	BRAINTREE, MA
0401	CHELSEA, MA
0401	EVERETT, MA
0401	QUINCY, MA
0401	REVERE, MA
0401	WEYMOUTH, MA
0402	SPRINGFIELD, MA
0403	WORCESTER, MA
0404	GLOUCESTER, MA
0405	NEW BEDFORD, MA
0406	PLYMOUTH, MA
0407	FALL RIVER, MA
0408	SALEM, MA
0409	PROVINCETOWN, MA
0410	BRIDGEPORT, CT
0411	HARTFORD, CT
0412	NEW HAVEN, CT
0413	GROTON, CT
0413	NEW LONDON, CT
0416	LAWRENCE, MA
0501	NEWPORT, RI

CODE #	Port Name
0502	PROVIDENCE, RI
0503	MELLVILLE, RI
0503	PORTSMOUTH, RI
0701	MORRISTOWN, NY
0701	OGDENSBURG, NY
0701	WADDINGTON, NY
0704	MASSENA, NY
0705	FORT COVINGTON, NY
0706	CAPE VINCENT, NY
0708	ALEXANDRIA BAY, NY
0711	CHATEAUGAY, NY
0712	CHAMPLAIN–ROUSES POINT, NY
0714	CLAYTON, NY
0715	TROUT RIVER, NY
0901	BUFFALO–NIAGARA FALLS, NY
0903	ROCHESTER, NY
0904	OSWEGO, NY
0905	SODUS POINT, NY
0906	SYRACUSE, NY
0907	UTICA, NY
4601	NEWARK, NJ
4602	PERTH AMBOY, NJ
4701	JFK
4770	JAMAICA, NY
1001	NEW YORK, NY
1001	ELIZABETH, NJ

CODE #	Port Name	CODE #	Port Name
1002	ALBANY, NY	1303	BALTIMORE, MD
1003	NEWARK, NJ	1304	CRISFIELD, MD
1004	PERTH AMBOY, NJ		
1072	DHL, JAMAICA, NY	5401	WASHINGTON, DC
1101	PHILADELPHIA, PA	5402	ALEXANDRIA, VA
1102	CHESTER, PA		
1103	CLAYMONT, DE	1401	NORFOLK, VA
1103	DELAWARE CITY, DE	1401	PORTSMOUTH, VA
1103	EDGEMOOR, DE	1402	NEWPORT NEWS, VA
1103	PIGEON POINT, DE	1402	YORK RIVER, VA
1103	REEDY POINT, DE	1404	APPOMATTOX RIVER, VA
1103	WILMINGTON, DE	1404	JAMES RIVER, VA
1104	PITTSBURGH, PA	1404	RICHMOND– PETERSBURG, VA
1105	BILLINGSPORT, NJ	1408	HOPEWELL, VA
1105	EAGLE POINT, NJ	1409	CHARLESTON, WV
1105	MANTUA CREEK, NJ	1410	FRONT ROYAL, VA
1105	PAULSBORO, NJ		
1105	THOMPSON POINT, NJ	1501	WILMINGTON, NC
1105	WESTVILLE, NJ	1502	GREENSBORO, NC
1106	SCRANTON, PA	1503	DURHAM, NC
1106	WILKES– BARRE/SCRANTON, PA	1506	REIDSVILLE, NC
1107	CAMDEN, NJ	1511	MOREHEAD CITY– BEAUFORT, NC
1107	DELAIR, NJ	1512	CHARLOTTE, NC
1107	PETTY ISLAND, NJ		
1108	PHILADELPHIA INT'L AIRPORT, PA	1601	CHARLESTON, SC
1109	HARRISBURG, PA	1602	GEORGETOWN, SC
1113	GLOUCESTER CITY, NJ	1603	GREENVILLE– SPARTANBURG, SC
1118	MARCUS HOOK, PA	1604	COLUMBIA, SC
1119	LEHIGH VALLEY PORT OF ENTRY, LEHIGH		
		1701	BRUNSWICK, GA
1301	ANNAPOLIS, MD		
1302	CAMBRIDGE, MD		

CODE #	Port Name
1703	SAVANNAH, GA
1704	ATLANTA, GA
5201	MIAMI, FL
5202	KEY WEST, FL
5203	DANIA, FL
5203	FORT LAUDERDALE, FL
5203	HOLLYWOOD, FL
5203	PORT EVERGLADES, FL
5204	WEST PALM BEACH, FL
5205	FORT PIERCE, FL
1801	PORT TAMPA, FL
1801	TAMPA, FL
1803	JACKSONVILLE, FL
1805	FERNANDINA BEACH, FL
1807	BOCA GRANDE, FL
1808	ORLANDO, FL
1814	ST. PETERSBURG, FL
1816	PORT CANAVERAL, FL
1818	PANAMA CITY, FL
1819	PENSACOLA, FL
1821	PORT MANATEE, FL
1901	MOBILE, AL
1901	THEODORE, AL
1902	GULFPORT, MS
1903	PASCAGOULA, MS
1904	BIRMINGHAM, AL
1910	HUNTSVILLE, AL
2001	MORGAN CITY, LA
2002	BELLE CHASSE, LA

CODE #	Port Name
2002	CONCESSION, LA
2002	GRETNA, LA
2002	HARVEY, LA
2002	INNER HARBOR, LA
2002	MARRERO, LA
2002	NAVIGATION CANAL, LA
2002	NEW ORLEANS, LA
2002	SEATRAIN LANDING, LA
2002	SOUTHPORT, LA
2002	WESTWEGO, LA
2003	LITTLE ROCK, AR
2004	BATON ROUGE, LA
2005	PORT SULPHUR, LA
2006	MEMPHIS, TN
2007	NASHVILLE, TN
2008	CHATTANOOGA, TN
2009	DESTREHAN, LA
2009	LULING, LA
2010	GRAMERCY, LA
2011	GREENVILLE, MS
2012	AVONDALE, LA
2013	ST. ROSE, LA
2014	GOOD HOPE, LA
2015	VICKSBURG, MS
2016	KNOXVILLE, TN
2017	LAKE CHARLES, LA
2018	SHREVEPORT–BOSSIER CITY, LA
2082	TRI–CITY USER FEE AIRPORT, BOUNTVILL
2095	FEDERAL EXPRESS, MEMPHIS, TN
2101	PORT ARTHUR, TX
2102	SABINE, TX

CODE #	Port Name	CODE #	Port Name
2103	ORANGE, TX	5507	SAN ANTONIO, TX
2104	BEAUMONT, TX	5582	MIDLAND INTERNATIONAL AIRPORT, TX
2104	PORT NECHES, TX		
	🚢	5583	FORT WORTH, TX
2301	BROWNSVILLE, TX		🚢
2301	CAMERON COUNTY, TX	2402	EL PASO, TX
2301	PORT ISABEL, TX	2402	YSLETA, TX
2302	DEL RIO, TX	2403	PRESIDIO, TX
2303	EAGLE PASS, TX	2404	FABENS, TX
2304	LAREDO, TX	2406	COLUMBUS, NM
2305	HIDALGO, TX	2407	ALBUQUERQUE, NM
2307	RIO GRANDE CITY, TX	2408	SANTA TERESA, NM
2309	PROGRESSO, TX		🚢
2310	ROMA, TX	2501	SAN DIEGO, CA
	🚢	2502	ANDRADE, CA
5301	BAYTOWN, TX	2503	CALEXICO, CA
5301	HOUSTON, TX	2504	SAN YSIDRO, CA
5306	TEXAS CITY, TX	2505	TECATE, CA
5310	GALVESTON, TX	2506	OTAY MESA STATION, CA
5311	FREEPORT, TX		
5312	CORPUS CHRISTI, TX	2507	CALEXICO–EAST, CA
5312	INGLESIDE TERMINAL, TX		🚢
5312	PORT ARANSAS, TX	2601	DOUGLAS, AZ
5313	PORT LAVACA, TX	2602	LUKEVILLE, AZ
	🚢	2603	NACO, AZ
5501	DALLAS–FORT WORTH, TX	2604	NOGALES, AZ
5501	FORT WORTH, TX	2605	PHOENIX, AZ
5502	AMARILLO, TX	2606	SASABE, AZ
5503	LUBBOCK, TX	2608	SAN LUIS, AZ
5504	OKLAHOMA CITY, OK	2609	TUCSON, AZ
5505	TULSA, OK		🚢
5506	AUSTIN, TX	2704	LOS ANGELES, CA
		2707	PORT SAN LUIS, CA

CODE #	Port Name	CODE #	Port Name
2709	HUNTINGTON BEACH, CA	2829	VALLEJO, CA
2709	LONG BEACH, CA	2830	BENICIA, CA
2709	NEWPORT BAY, CA	2830	CARQUINEZ STRAIT, CA
2709	SAN PEDRO, CA	2830	PORT COSTA, CA
2711	EL SEGUNDO, CA	2831	AVON, CA
2712	VENTURA, CA	2831	SACRAMENTO POINT, CA
2713	PORT HUENEME, CA	2831	SUISUN BAY, CA
2715	CAPITAN, CA	2831	SUISUN SLOUGH, CA
2719	ESTERO BAY, CA	2833	RENO, NV
2719	MORRO, CA		
2722	LAS VEGAS, NV	2901	ASTORIA, OR
		2902	NEWPORT, OR
2802	EUREKA, CA	2902	TOLEDO, OR
2803	FRESNO, CA	2903	COOS BAY, OR
2805	MONTEREY, CA	2903	EMPIRE, OR
2809	SAN FRANCISCO, CA	2903	MILLINGTON, OR
2810	STOCKTON, CA	2903	NORTH BEND, OR
2811	OAKLAND, CA	2904	LINNTON, OR
2812	RICHMOND, CA	2904	PORTLAND, OR
2813	ALAMEDA, CA	2905	LONGVIEW, WA
2815	CROCKETT, CA	2907	BOISE, ID
2816	SACRAMENTO, CA	2908	VANCOUVER, WA
2820	MARTINEZ, CA	2909	KALAMA, WA
2821	REDWOOD CITY, CA	2981	KLAMATH FALLS, OR
2827	SELBY, CA	2982	MEDFORD, OR
2828	ANTIOCH, CA		
2828	MAYBERRY SLOUGH, CA	3001	POINT WELLS, WA
2828	PITTSBURG, CA	3001	SEATTLE, WA
2828	SAN JOAQUIN RIVER, CA	3002	TACOMA, WA
2829	MARE ISLAND STRAIT, CA	3003	ABERDEEN–HOQUIAM, WA
2829	OLEUM, CA	3003	GRAYS HARBOR, WA
2829	SAN PABLO BAY, CA	3004	BLAINE, WA
2829	SAN PABLO, CA	3005	BELLINGHAM, WA

CODE #	Port Name	CODE #	Port Name
3006	EVERETT, WA	3124	PELICAN, AK
3007	PORT ANGELES, WA	3125	SAND POINT, AK
3008	PORT TOWNSEND, WA	3126	ANCHORAGE, AK
3009	SUMAS, WA	3127	KODIAK, AK
3010	ANACORTES, WA		
3011	NIGHTHAWK, WA	3201	HONOLULU, HI
3012	DANVILLE, WA	3201	PEARL HARBOR, HI
3013	FERRY, WA	3202	HILO, HI
3014	FRIDAY HARBOR, WA	3203	KAHULUI, HI
3015	BOUNDARY, WA		
3016	LAURIER, WA		
3017	POINT ROBERTS, WA	3301	RAYMOND, MT
3019	OROVILLE, WA	3302	EASTPORT, ID
3020	FRONTIER, WA	3303	SALT LAKE CITY, UT
3022	SPOKANE, WA	3304	GREAT FALLS, MT
3023	LYNDEN, WA	3305	BUTTE, MT
3025	METALINE FALLS, WA	3306	TURNER, MT
3026	OLYMPIA, WA	3307	DENVER, CO
3027	NEAH BAY, WA	3308	PORTHILL, ID
3081	YAKIMA, WA	3309	SCOBEY, MT
3082	MOSES, WA	3310	SWEETGRASS, MT
		3312	WHITETAIL, MT
		3316	PIEGAN, MT
3101	JUNEAU, AK	3317	OPHEIM, MT
3102	HERRING BAY, AK	3318	ROOSVILLE, MT
3102	KETCHIKAN, AK	3319	MORGAN, MT
3102	WARD COVE, AK	3321	WHITLASH, MT
3103	SKAGWAY, AK	3322	DEL BONITA, MT
3104	ALCAN, AK		
3105	WRANGELL, AK		
3106	DALTON CACHE, AK	3401	PEMBINA, ND
3107	VALDEZ, AK	3402	NOYES, MN
3111	FAIRBANKS, AK	3403	PORTAL, ND
3112	PETERSBURG, AK	3404	NECHE, ND
3115	SITKA, AK	3405	ST. JOHN, ND

CODE #	Port Name
3406	NORTHGATE, ND
3407	WALHALLA, ND
3408	HANNAH, ND
3409	SARLES, ND
3410	AMBROSE, ND
3413	ANTLER, ND
3414	SHERWOOD, ND
3415	HANSBORO, ND
3416	MAIDA, ND
3417	FORTUNA, ND
3419	WESTHOPE, ND
3420	NOONAN, ND
3421	CARBURY, ND
3422	DUNSEITH, ND
3423	OAK ISLAND, MN
3423	WARROAD, MN
3424	BAUDETTE, MN
3425	PINECREEK, MN
3426	ROSEAU, MN
3501	MINNEAPOLIS–ST. PAUL, MN
3601	DULUTH, MN
3602	ASHLAND, WI
3604	INTERNATIONAL FALLS– RANIER, MN
3608	SUPERIOR, WI
3613	GRAND PORTAGE, MN
3614	SILVER BAY, MN
3614	TACONITE, MN
3701	MILWAUKEE, WI
3702	MARINETTE, WI

CODE #	Port Name
3702	MENOMINEE, MI
3703	DEPERE, WI
3703	GREEN BAY, WI
3706	MANITOWOC, WI
3707	SHEBOYGAN, WI
3708	KENOSHA, WI
3708	RACINE, WI
3801	CALUMET HARBOR, IL
3801	DETROIT,MI
3801	ECORSE, MI
3801	RIVER ROUGE, MI
3801	RIVERVIEW, MI
3801	TRENTON, MI
3801	WYANDOTTE, MI
3802	BLACK RIVER, MI
3802	MARYSVILLE, MI
3802	PORT HURON, MI
3802	ST. CLAIR, MI
3803	MUNISING, MI
3803	PORT INLAND, MI
3803	SAULT STE. MARIE, MI
3804	BANGOR, MI
3804	CARROLLTON, MI
3804	ESSEXVILLE, MI
3804	FLINT, MI
3804	SAGINAW–BAY CITY– FLINT, MI
3805	BATTLE CREEK, MI
3806	GRAND RAPIDS, MI
3808	ESCANABA, MI
3809	MARQUETTE, MI
3814	ALGONAC, MI
3814	ROBERTS LANDING, MI
3815	MANISTEE, MI
3815	MUSKEGON, MI

CODE #	Port Name	CODE #	Port Name
3816	GRAND HAVEN, MI	4106	ERIE, PA
3818	CALCITE, MI	4108	ASHTABULA, OH
3818	ROGERS CITY, MI	4109	CONNEAUT, OH
3819	DETOUR, MI	4110	INDIANAPOLIS, IN
3820	MACKINAC ISLAND, MI	4111	FAIRPORT, OH
3842	PRESQUE ISLE, MN	4112	AKRON, OH
3843	ALPENA, MI	4115	LOUISVILLE, KY
3843	BAYSHORE, MI	4116	EVANSVILLE, IN
3843	STONEPORT, MI	4116	OWENSBORO, KY
3844	FERRYSBURG, MI	4117	HURON, OH
		4121	LORAIN, OH
		4181	WILMINGTON, OH
3901	CALUMET HARBOR, IL	4183	FORT WAYNE, IN
3901	CHICAGO, IL	4184	LEXINGTON, KY
3901	CHICAGO RIVER, IL		
3901	LOCKPORT, IL		
3901	WAUKEGAN HARBOR, IL	4501	KANSAS CITY, MO
3902	PEORIA, IL	4502	ST. JOSEPH, MO
3903	OMAHA, NE	4503	ST. LOUIS, MO
3904	EAST CHICAGO, IN	4504	WICHITA, KS
3905	GARY, IN	4505	SPRINGFIELD, MO
3905	MICHIGAN CITY HARBOR, IN		
3907	DES MOINES, IA	5101	CHARLOTTE AMALIE, VI
3908	DAVENPORT, IA	5102	CRUZ BAY, VI
3908	MOLINE, IL	5103	CORAL BAY, VI
3908	ROCK ISLAND, IL	5104	CHRISTIANSTED, VI
		5105	FREDERIKSTED, VI
4101	CLEVELAND, OH		
4102	CINCINNATI, OH	4901	AGUADILLA, PR
4102	LAWRENCEBURG, IN	4904	FAJARDO, PR
4103	COLUMBUS, OH	4905	GUANICA, PR
4104	DAYTON, OH	4906	HUMACAO, PR
4105	SANDUSKY, OH	4907	MAYAGUEZ, PR
4105	TOLEDO, OH	4908	PONCE, PR

CODE #	Port Name
4909	SAN JUAN, PR
4911	JOBOS, PR
4912	GUAYANILLA, PR

Current Port List, see District Port Codes - grouped by geographical region. On right side of page at this web site:

http://www.cbp.gov/xp/cgov/toolbox/ports/

Innocent Passage – UN Law of the Sea

Part 2 –Territorial Sea, Sections 3, and Section 4 – Contiguous Zone

Part 3 – Straits

Part 4 – Archipelagic

Only the material from Part 2, Section 3 is included here. Part 2, Section 4 pertains to material for the Contiguous Zone, and the material pertaining to Straits, and Archipelagic States I have not included as it is nearly identical.

Part II
TERRITORIAL SEA AND CONTIGUOUS ZONE

SECTION 3. INNOCENT PASSAGE IN THE TERRITORIAL SEA

SUBSECTION A. RULES APPLICABLE TO ALL SHIPS

Article17

Right of innocent passage

Subject to this Convention, ships of all States, whether coastal, or land-locked, enjoy the right of innocent passage through the territorial sea.

Article18

Meaning of passage

1. Passage means navigation through the territorial sea for the purpose of:

(a) traversing that sea without entering internal waters, or calling at a roadstead, or port facility outside internal waters;, or

(b) proceeding to, or from internal waters, or a call at such roadstead, or port facility.

2. Passage shall be continuous, and expeditious. However, passage includes stopping, and anchoring, but only in so far as the same are incidental to, ordinary navigation, or are rendered necessary by *force majeure*, or distress, or for the purpose of rendering assistance to persons, ships, or aircraft in danger, or distress.

Article19

Meaning of innocent passage

1. Passage is innocent so long as it is not prejudicial to the peace, good, order, or security of the coastal State. Such passage shall take place in conformity with this Convention, and with other rules of international law.

2. Passage of a foreign ship shall be considered to be prejudicial to the peace, good, order, or security of the coastal State if in the territorial sea it engages in any of the following activities:

any threat, or use of force against the sovereignty, territorial integrity, or political independence of the coastal State, or in any other manner in violation of the principles of international law embodied in the Charter of the United Nations;

any exercise, or practice with weapons of any kind;

any act aimed at collecting information to the prejudice of the defense, or security of the coastal State;

any act of propaganda aimed at affecting the defense, or security of the coastal State;

(e) the launching, landing, or taking on board of any aircraft;

(f) the launching, landing, or taking on board of any military device;

(g) the loading, or unloading of any commodity, currency, or person contrary to the customs, fiscal, immigration, or sanitary laws, and regulations of the coastal State;

(h) any act of willful, and serious pollution contrary to this Convention;

(i) any fishing activities;

(j) the carrying out of research, or survey activities;

(k) any act aimed at interfering with any systems of communication, or any other facilities, or installations of the coastal State;

(l) any other activity not having a direct bearing on passage.

Article20

Submarines, and other underwater vehicles

In the territorial sea, submarines, and other underwater vehicles are required to navigate on the surface, and to show their flag.

Article21

Laws, and regulations of the coastal State relating to innocent passage

1. The coastal State may adopt laws, and regulations, in conformity with the provisions of this Convention, and other rules of international law, relating to innocent passage through the territorial sea, in respect of all, or any of the following:

(a) the safety of navigation, and the regulation of maritime traffic;

(b) the protection of navigational aids, and facilities, and other facilities, or installations;

(c) the protection of cables, and pipelines;

(d) the conservation of the living resources of the sea;

(e) the prevention of infringement of the fisheries laws, and regulations of the coastal State;

(f) the preservation of the environment of the coastal State, and the prevention, reduction, and control of pollution thereof;

(g) marine scientific research, and hydrographic surveys;

(h) the prevention of infringement of the customs, fiscal, immigration, or sanitary laws, and regulations of the coastal State.

2. Such laws, and regulations shall not apply to the design, construction, manning, or equipment of foreign ships unless they are giving effect to generally accepted international rules, or standards.

3. The coastal State shall give due publicity to all such laws, and regulations.

Foreign ships exercising the right of innocent passage through the territorial sea shall comply with all such laws, and regulations, and all generally accepted international regulations relating to the prevention of collisions at sea.

Article22

Sea lanes, and traffic separation schemes in the territorial sea

1. The coastal State may, where necessary having regard to the safety of navigation, require foreign ships exercising the right of innocent passage through its territorial sea to use such sea lanes, and traffic separation schemes as it may designate, or prescribe for the regulation of the passage of ships.

2. In particular, tankers, nuclear-powered ships, and ships carrying nuclear, or other inherently dangerous, or noxious substances, or materials may be required to confine their passage to such sea lanes.

3. In the designation of sea lanes, and the prescription of traffic separation schemes under this article, the coastal State shall take into account:

(a) the recommendations of the competent international, organization;

(b) any channels customarily used for international navigation;

(c) the special characteristics of particular ships, and channels; and

(d) the density of traffic.

The coastal State shall clearly indicate such sea lanes, and traffic separation schemes on charts to which due publicity shall be given.

Article23

Foreign nuclear-powered ships, and ships carrying nuclear or other inherently dangerous, or noxious substances

Foreign nuclear-powered ships, and ships carrying nuclear, or other inherently dangerous, or noxious substances shall, when exercising the right of innocent passage through the territorial sea, carry documents, and observe special precautionary measures established for such ships by international agreements.

Article24

Duties of the coastal State

1. The coastal State shall not hamper the innocent passage of foreign ships through the territorial sea except in accordance with this Convention. In particular, in the application of this Convention, or of any laws, or regulations adopted in conformity with this Convention, the coastal State shall not:

(a) impose requirements on foreign ships which have the practical effect of denying, or impairing the right of innocent passage;, or

(b) discriminate in form, or in fact against the ships of any State, or against ships carrying cargoes to, from, or on behalf of any State.

2. The coastal State shall give appropriate publicity to any danger to navigation, of which it has knowledge, within its territorial sea.

Article25

Rights of protection of the coastal State

1. The coastal State may take the necessary steps in its territorial sea to prevent passage which is not innocent.

2. In the case of ships proceeding to internal waters, or a call at a port facility outside internal waters, the coastal State also has the right to take the necessary steps to prevent any breach of the conditions to which admission of those ships to internal waters, or such a call is subject.

3. The coastal State may, without discrimination in form, or in fact among foreign ships, suspend temporarily in specified areas of its territorial sea the innocent passage of foreign ships if such suspension is essential for the protection of its security, including weapons exercises. Such suspension shall take effect only after having been duly published.

Article26

Charges which may be levied upon foreign ships

1. No charge may be levied upon foreign ships by reason only of their passage through the territorial sea.

2. Charges may be levied upon a foreign ship passing through the territorial sea as payment only for specific services rendered to the ship. These charges shall be levied without discrimination.

SUBSECTION B. RULES APPLICABLE TO

MERCHANT SHIPS, and GOVERNMENT SHIPS

OPERATED FOR COMMERCIAL PURPOSES

Article27

Criminal jurisdiction on board a foreign ship

1. The criminal jurisdiction of the coastal State should not be exercised on board a foreign ship passing through the territorial sea to arrest any person, or to conduct any investigation in connection with any crime committed on board the ship during its passage, save only in the following cases:

(a) if the consequences of the crime extend to the coastal State;

(b) if the crime is of a kind to disturb the peace of the country, or the good, order of the territorial sea;

(c) if the assistance of the local authorities has been requested by the master of the ship, or by a diplomatic agent, or consular officer of the flag State;, or

(d) if such measures are necessary for the suppression of illicit traffic in narcotic drugs, or psychotropic substances.

2. The above provisions do not affect the right of the coastal State to take any steps authorized by its laws for the purpose of an arrest, or investigation on board a foreign ship passing through the territorial sea after leaving internal waters.

3. In the cases provided for in paragraphs 1, and 2, the coastal State shall, if the master so requests, notify a diplomatic agent, or consular officer of the flag State before taking any steps, and shall facilitate contact between such agent, or officer, and the ship's crew. In cases of emergency this notification may be communicated while the measures are being taken.

In considering whether, or in what manner an arrest should be made, the local authorities shall have due regard to the interests of navigation.

5. Except as provided in Part XII, or with respect to violations of laws, and regulations adopted in accordance with Part V, the coastal State may not take any steps on board a foreign ship passing through the territorial sea to arrest any person, or to conduct any investigation in connection with any crime committed before the ship entered the territorial sea, if the

ship, proceeding from a foreign port, is only passing through the territorial sea without entering internal waters.

Article28

Civil jurisdiction in relation to foreign ships

1. The coastal State should not stop, or divert a foreign ship passing through the territorial sea for the purpose of exercising civil jurisdiction in relation to a person on board the ship.

2. The coastal State may not levy execution against, or arrest the ship for the purpose of any civil proceedings, save only in respect of obligations, or liabilities assumed, or incurred by the ship itself in the course, or for the purpose of its voyage through the waters of the coastal State.

3. Paragraph 2 is without prejudice to the right of the coastal State, in accordance with its laws, to levy execution against, or to arrest, for the purpose of any civil proceedings, a foreign ship lying in the territorial sea, or passing through the territorial sea after leaving internal waters.

Territorial, Contiguous & EEZ Claims

By Country, in Nautical Miles

Country [84]	Territorial Sea	Contiguous Zone
Albania	12	
Algeria	12	24
Angola	12	24
Antigua, and Barbuda	12	24
Argentina	12	24
Australia	12 [85]	24
Bahamas	12	
Bahrain	12	
Bangladesh	12	18
Barbados	12	
Belgium	12	24
Belize	12 [86]	

Country [84]	Territorial Sea	Contiguous Zone
Benin	200	
Brazil	12	24
Brunei	12	
Bulgaria	12	24
Cambodia	12	24
Cameroon	12 [87]	
Canada	12	24
Cape Verde	12	24
Chile	12	24
People's Republic of China	12	24
Republic of China	12	
Colombia	12	
Comoros	12	
Congo	200	
Cook Islands	12	
Costa Rica	12	
Cote d'Ivoire	12	
Croatia	12	
Cuba	12	24
Cyprus	12	24
Democratic People's Republic of Korea	12	50 [88]
Democratic Republic of the Congo	12	

[84] Wikipedia
http://en.wikipedia.org/wiki/Territorial_waters

[85] Australia: The territorial sea boundaries between the islands of Aubusi, Boigu, and Moimi, and Papua New Guinea, and the islands of Dauan, Kaumag, and Saibai, and Papua New Guinea, together with such other portion of the outer limit of the territorial sea of Saibai are determined by a treaty with Papua New Guinea. The territorial seas of the islands known as Anchor Cay, Aubusi Island, Black Rocks, Boigu Island, Bramble Cay, Dauan Island, Deliverance Island, East Cay, Kaumag Island, Kerr Islet, Moimi Island, Pearce Cay, Saibai Island, Turnagain Island, and Turu Cay do not extend beyond 3 nautical miles from the baselines.

[86] Belize: 3 nautical miles limit applies from the mouth of Sarstoon River to Ranguana Caye.

[87] Cameroon: See article 45 of Law 96-06 of 18 January 1996 on the revision of the Constitution of 2 June 1972.

[88] Fifty nautical mile (93 km) military zone. Army Command Announcement of 1 August 1977.

Country [84]	Territorial Sea	Contiguous Zone
Denmark	12 [89]	
Djibouti	12	24
Dominica	12	24
Dominican Republic	6	24
Ecuador	200 [90]	
Egypt	12	24
El Salvador	200	
Equatorial Guinea	12	
Eritrea	12	
Estonia	12 [91]	
Fiji	12	
Finland	12 [92]	14

Country [84]	Territorial Sea	Contiguous Zone
France	12	24
Gabon	12	24
Gambia	12	18
Georgia	12	
Germany	12	
Ghana	12	24
Greece	6 [93]	
Grenada	12	
Guatemala	12	
Guinea	12	
Guinea-Bissau	12	
Guyana	12	
Haiti	12	24
Honduras	12	24
Iceland	12	
India	12 [94]	24
Indonesia	12	
Iran	12	24
Iraq	12	
Ireland	12	
Israel	12	
Italy	12	
Jamaica	12	24
Japan	12 [95]	24

[89] Denmark: Act No. 200 of 7 April 1999 on the delimitation of the territorial sea does not apply to the Faroe Islands, and Greenland but may become effective by Royal Decree for those parts of the Kingdom of Denmark with the amendments dictated by the special conditions prevailing in the Faroe Islands, and Greenland. As far as Greenland is concerned, the outer limit of the external territorial waters may be measured at a distance shorter than 12 nautical miles from the baselines.

[90] Ecuador: The 200 nautical miles limit is in effect only between the continental territorial sea of Ecuador, and its insular territorial sea around the Galápagos Islands.

[91] Estonia: In some parts of the Gulf of Finland, defined by coordinates.

[92] Finland: Extends, with certain exceptions, to 12 nautical miles, unless defined by geographical coordinates. In the Gulf of Finland, the outer limit of the territorial sea shall at no place be closer to the midline than 3 nautical miles, according to the Act amending the Act on the Limits of the Territorial Waters of Finland (981/95).

[93] Greece: 10-nautical-mile (18.5 km) limit applies for the purpose of regulating civil aviation.

[94] India: 12 nautical mile limit includes Andaman, Nicobar, and Lakshadweep.

[95] Japan: 3 nautical mile limit applies to the Soya Strait, the Tsugaru Strait, the eastern, and western channels of the Korea Strait, and the Osumi Straits only.

Country [84]	Territorial Sea	Contiguous Zone
Jordan	3	
Kenya	12	
Kiribati	12	
Kuwait	12	
Latvia	12	
Lebanon	12	
Liberia	200	
Libya	12	
Lithuania	12	
Madagascar	12	24
Malaysia	12	
Maldives	12	24
Malta	12	24
Marshall Islands	12	24
Mauritania	12	24
Mauritius	12	
Mexico	12	24
Micronesia	12	
Monaco	12	
Morocco	12	24
Mozambique	12	24
Myanmar	12	24
Namibia	12	24
Nauru	12	24
Netherlands	12	
New Zealand	12 [96]	24
Nicaragua	12	24
Nigeria	12	
Niue	12	
Norway	12	24

Country [84]	Territorial Sea	Contiguous Zone
Oman	12	24
Pakistan	12	24
Palau	3	
Panama	12	24
Papua New Guinea	12 [97]	
Peru	200 [98]	
Philippines	[99]	
Poland	12	
Portugal	12	24
Qatar	12	24
Republic of Korea	12	24
Romania	12	24
Russia	12	24
Saint Kitts, and Nevis	12	24
Saint Lucia	12	24
Saint Vincent, and the Grenadines	12	24
Samoa	12	24
São Tomé, and Príncipe	12	

[96] New Zealand: 12 nautical mile limit includes Tokelau.

[97] Papua New Guinea: 3 nautical miles in certain areas.

[98] Peru: The 200 nautical mile territorial sea is called 'Maritime Dominion' in article 54 of the 1993 Constitution: " ...In its maritime dominion, Peru exercises sovereignty, and jurisdiction, without prejudice to the freedoms of international communication, in accordance with the law, and the treaties ratified by the State... "

[99] Philippines (Rectangle defined by coordinates. Claim extends beyond 12 nautical miles).

Country [84]	Terri-torial Sea	Conti-guous Zone
Singapore	3	
Saudi Arabia	12	18
Senegal	12	24
Seychelles	12	24
Sierra Leone	12	24
Slovenia	100	
Solomon Islands	12	
Somalia	200	
South Africa	12	24
Spain	12	24
Sri Lanka	12	24
Syria	12	24
Sudan	12	18
Suriname	12	
Sweden	12	
Syria	12	
Thailand	12	
Timor-Leste	12	
Togo	30	
Tonga	12	
Thailand	12	24
Timor East	12	24
Trinidad & Tobago	12	24
Tunisia	12	24
Turkey	6 [101]	

Country [84]	Terri-torial Sea	Conti-guous Zone
Tuvalu	12	24
Ukraine	12	
United Arab Emirates	12	
United Kingdom	12 [102]	
United Republic of Tanzania	12	
United States of America	12	24
Uruguay	12	24
Vanuatu	12	24
Venezuela	12	15
Vietnam	12	24
Yemen	12	24

Contiguous Zones – no entry in the table means, that the country has no declared contiguous zone.

[100] Slovenia (DLM means that "the national legislation establishes the limits of a given zone only by reference to the delimitation of maritime boundaries with adjacent, or opposite States, or to a median (equidistant) line in the absence of a maritime boundary delimitation agreement")

[101] Turkey: 6 nautical miles in the Aegean Sea, 12 nautical miles in the Black Sea.

[102] United Kingdom: Also 3 nautical miles. (3 nautical miles in Anguilla, Guernsey, British Indian Ocean Territory, British Virgin Islands, Gibraltar, Monserrat, and Pitcairn; 12 nautical miles in United Kingdom, Jersey, Bermuda, Cayman Islands, Falkland Islands, Isle of Man, Saint Helena, and Dependencies, South Georgia, South Sandwich Islands, and Turks, and Caicos Islands).

Duty Free Ports

Duty Free is not necessarily no VAT.

Duty Free Zones. Some of the listings in Duty Free Zones actually belong in a *Port List*.	No Restrictions[104]	Geographic Zone.[105]	VAT[106]
India. Goa		A	
Malaysia. Port Kelang		A	
Malaysia. Labuan, Victoria		A	
Malaysia. Langkawi		A	
Mauritius. Port Luis		A	
Thailand. Phuket (in future)		A	
Canary Island. Las Palmas		AF	
Canary Islands. Tenerif		AF	
Egypt. Port Said, Port Suez		AF	
Egypt. Safaga		AF	
Liberia. Monrovia		AF	
Spanish Morocco. Ceuta		AF	N
Spanish Morocco. Mellila		AF	N
Togo		AF	
Jordan. Aqaba		AR	
UAE. Dubai?		AR	
Yemen. Aden?		AR	
Aruba, Oranjestad		C	

---

[103] Zones or Ports: used by & available to Cruisers. There are likely errors in this interpretation.

[104] Few or none

[105] Asia, Europe, America, Africa, Arabia, Caribbean, Pacific

[106] Generally only in EU

Duty Free Zones. Some of the listings in Duty Free Zones actually belong in a *Port List*.	No Restrictions[108]	Geographic Zone. [109]	VAT[110]
Bahamas. Freeport, Nassau		C	
Barbados		C	
Belize. Belize City		C	
Cayman Islands	YES	C	
Columbia. Isla San Andreas	YES	C	
Curaçao. Willemstad		C	
Dominican Republic Port of Punta Caucedo		C	
Martinique. Saint Lucia, Saint Pierre	YES	C	
Mexico. Cancun		C	
St. Barts. Gustavia		C	
St. Lucia at Pointe Seraphine		C	
St. Martin		C	
U.S. Virgin Islands	YES	C	
Costa Rica. Golfito		CA	
Mexico. Baja Calif. ?	YES	CA	
Mexico. Puerto Mexico		CA	
Mexico. Salina Cruz		CA	
Nicaragua. Managua		CA	
Panama. Colon		CA	
Denmark. Copenhagen		E	

---

[107] Zones or Ports: used by & available to Cruisers. There are likely errors in this interpretation

[108] Few or none

[109] Asia, Europe, America, Africa, Arabia, Caribbean, Pacific

[110] Generally only in EU

Duty Free Zones. Some of the listings in Duty Free Zones actually belong in a *Port List*. [111]	No Restrictions[112]	Geographic Zone. [113]	VAT[114]
Finland. Hanko		E	
Germany. Bremen, Cuxhaven, Deggendorf, Duisburg, Emden, Hamburg, and Kiel		E	
Gibralter	YES	E	N
Ireland. Ringaskiddy		E	
Latvia. Riga, Ventspils		E	
Lithuania. Klaipedia		E	
Malta		E	
UK. Isle of Man		E	
Ukraine. Odessa		E	
Bermuda. Hamilton		NA	
Argentina. Ushuaia		SA	
Brazil. Manaus (1000 miles up the Amazon)		SA	
Chile. Arica		SA	
Chile. Iqueque		SA	
Ecuador. Galapagos Islands	YES	SA	
Paraguay. Ciudad del Este		SA	
Venezuela. Isla de Margarita, Porlamar		SA	

---

[111] Zones or Ports: used by & available to Cruisers. There are likely errors in this interpretation

[112] Few or none

[113] Asia, Europe, America, Africa, Arabia, Caribbean, Pacific

[114] Generally only in EU

Duty Free Zones. Some of the listings in Duty Free Zones actually belong in a *Port List.* [115]	No Restrictions[116]	Geographic Zone. [117]	VAT[118]
Indonesia. Sabang, Wei Island		WP	
Tonga & Vavau		WP	
United States. Guam	YES	WP	
Vanuatu. Port Vila, Island of Efate		WP	
China. Hong Kong.	YES	WP, A	
China. Macao	YES	WP, A	
Philippines. Subic Bay		WP, A	
Singapore		WP, A	
Philippines. Zamboanga		WP,A	

Only a few of these Duty Free zones have no restrictions. In any event, in most cases they can serve as a place where you can have parts, or other materials shipped, and pick up for your boat without being involved in duty being owed.

A = Asia, AF = Africa, C = Caribbean, CA = Central America, E = Europe, NA = North America, SA = South America, WP = Western Pacific.

---

[115] Zones or Ports used by & available to Cruisers. There are likely errors in this interpretation.

[116] Few or none.

[117] Asia, Europe, America, Africa, Arabia, Caribbean, Pacific

[118] Generally only in EU.

Capt. Mike's – General Standing Orders

1. The orders listed below must be read, and are normally signed in the log by each deck officer before taking his first watch on the bridge. This is a <u>small</u> ship. If you have the watch, you are that person!

2. When alone on the bridge you should always keep in mind that the time for taking action for the vessel's safety is <u>while there is still time</u> to do so.

3. In an emergency, **do not hesitate** to ***<u>slow</u>*** down, ***<u>stop</u>***, or ***<u>go astern</u>***. Try to call me in time to make the bridge. Use the horn. The decision <u>will</u> fall to you. If needed, make it!

4. The watch officer should be on the bridge at all times, and should never leave the bridge until relieved, or when it is **known for certain** that no close quarters situation can occur before their return. A few minutes in, open waters, <u>none</u> in close.

5. When relieving the current watch, the relieving officer should acquaint himself with the vessel's position, course, and speed, weather conditions (present, and expected), and obtain any pertinent information the watch being relieved may have to pass on: vessels encountered, amount of traffic, engine-bilge conditions, or other dangers.

6. As watch officer of this vessel, you are when on duty, expected to keep a good lookout, and see that your assistants do the same. You are the eyes, and ears of the ship. The safety of it, and all aboard, rest in your hands. Unnecessary conversation is not conducive to keeping a proper watch.

7. When visibility becomes poor, less than 2 miles, or if you anticipate that, it may become poor because of fog, mist, rain, snow, or any other reason, call me. In the meantime, **post additional lookouts** as warranted, *consider* putting the vessel on hand steering, and start the foghorn, turn on running lights.

8. Be sure the lookout, which is most likely you, is thoroughly familiar with his duties, and keeps alert. Our running lights are to **protect us** from being rammed, and sunk. When on: they should be checked every hour. Do not put yourself in danger of going overboard while checking the lights. Be certain they are each working.

9. It is good practice to use the radar, and plot targets at all times, even in clear weather.

10. Call me at any time – if in doubt – but do it in time. Better too soon, than too late. Call me if the weather worsens, or you think it may be necessary to slow down.

11. In poor visibility, the radar <u>must</u> be turned on. Use no more than 4–6 miles range for spotting small targets. Do not use the longer ranges except for brief periods. 3, sometimes 1 1/2 mile ranges are best for small targets.

12. Do not let the vessel pound. If you think she will pound, or shows a tendency to pound, slow down and, or alter course *__slightly__*, and *if necessary* call me.

13. This vessel is to be put on hand steering, prior to any close quarters situation with any other vessel, or, near(100–150 yards) ANY other fixed dangers, buoys, rocks, etc.

14. Give passing vessels a wide berth. Don't try to bluff others out of their *right-of-way*. At sea, keep at least 1 mile off passing vessels if possible, more if you think necessary. Call me for meeting, or crossing situations of less than 2 miles for slow moving vessels, and 3–4 miles if they are fast, or big.

15. At night, or during poor visibility, do not come within 1 1/2 miles (in front, side, or back) of <u>any tug</u> with long tow. 3 vertical white lights, forward, a yellow over white at the stern. Long tows are to be treated as **extremely** dangerous. Call me immediately, if in doubt.

16. At ranges exceeding our running lights. Turn on the searchlight for fast moving large vessels, or tugs with tow (point at them), when at a distance of 6–8 miles. Leave on for about 2–4 minutes. At a distance of 3–4 miles do this again for about 1–2 minutes. Let them know someone is out there. Avoid running the searchlight near other vessels.

17. If you think a near collision situation is **developing**, don't hesitate to get on the VHF radio, channels 13 & 16, and warn the other vessel off. Use the searchlight (not into his pilothouse), to assure he is aware of who is making the noise on the radio.

18. Watch out for small craft, and fishing vessels. Many do not carry proper lights. If you encounter a fishing fleet, call me.

19. Use the radar, fathometer, and GPS to constantly to verify our position. If water depths approach 20 fathoms, or less, call me.

20. If you note a discrepancy between what you believe is our proper location, and that which the radar, depth finder, or GPS indicate, call me.

21. If you find any indication that the vessel is headed into danger, call me.

22. In clear weather, use every practical opportunity to **practice radar plotting** the tracks of other vessels. Learn to accurately estimate the closest point of approach (CPA).

23. At night, lights, which degrade the night vision of the lookout(s) must be suppressed. Every effort should be made to keep extraneous lights to a minimum. Use colored flashlights (red, or blue) for reading charts, and instruments, raiding the pantry, etc. Night-scopes blind the user. The Red sidelight has the least impact on the night vision scope.

24. Lights from the radar, chart plotter, fish finders, etc, should be lowered to the lowest brilliance setting which still allows them to be seen. Navigation lights should be screened to prevent the masthead light from showing on the forward deck. Similar measures for the sidelights, and stern light.

25. Especially if you are alone, do not take any action, which might place you in danger, such as going near where you might fall overboard. If needed, ask for assistance.

26. Certain equipment belongs to the Captain. Do not turn off running lights, or make changes to settings without permission, to the radar, depth finder, or GPS.

27. There are no private mistakes aboard a vessel at sea. The Ship, and everyone aboard will share in the outcome.

28. The Captain's job is to control mistakes, and extricate the ship from any that happen. Bring them to me before it is <u>too</u> late.

29. You <u>will not die</u> from being chewed out. It is just part of the process of learning. But, if you hesitate to act, or call me in a timely fashion, you might expire in a cold sea, along with everyone aboard. Keep that in mind.

30. The "lady with the green eye's", who lives in the deep, is always out to kill you, and unlike you, she never sleeps, daydreams, or makes a mistake!!

You can live to be an old sailor.

Stay alert. Never make the same mistake twice.

Bibliography

General

A Captain's Guide to: Transiting the Panama Canal in a Small Vessel, by David W. Wilson. 1999

Chapman Piloting & Seamanship ISBN 158816232X

Farwell's Rules of the Nautical Road. Craig H. Allen.

Offshore Sailing: 200 Essential Passagemaking Tips. By Bill Seifert.

The Voyagers Handbook. Beth Leonard.

Merchant Marine Officers' Handbook. 5th Ed.

Law for Yachtsmen. 1952. Harold Dudley Greeley. LC 52-6340

Shipmaster's Handbook on Ship's Business. Ben Martin. ISBN 87033-098-5. Second Ed. 087033378X

Recommended Reading List

The Language of Sailors

When a Loose Cannon Flogs a Dead Horse, There's the Devil to Pay: Seafaring Words in Everyday Speech. By Olivia A. Isil.

Plymouth Naval Sayings page

http://tinyurl.com/2wemcb [lix]

Note: modern English owes much to the Old Mariners. As author Seth Lerer, "Inventing English" argues, Middle English effectively became Modern English at the time that people began to speak in the way we would call *Pirate English*.

One Hand for Yourself, One for the Ship. Tristan Jones

New Zealand Mariners Handbook. Ed. Tim Ridge

Empire of Blue Water. Stephan Talty. Captain Morgan's Great Pirate Army.

Dennis L. Noble. Lifeboat Sailors: Inside the Coast Guard's Small Boat Stations. Washington, D.C.: Brassey's, 2000.

Dennis L. Noble. The Rescue of the Gale Runner: Death, Heroism, and the U.S. Coast Guard. Gainesville: University Press of Florida, 2002.

Dennis Noble. Rescued By the U.S. Coast Guard: Great Acts of

Heroism Since 1878. Annapolis: Naval Institute Press, 200

Advanced Sailing. Tony Gibbs.

How Weather Works, and Why. Bob Lynott. ISBN 0-9618077-1-7

Outfitting. Practical Sailor.

Psychology of Sailing. The sea's effects on mind, and body. Michael Stadler. ISBN 0-87742-963-4

Yachtsman's Emergency Handbook. N. Hollander.

The Ocean Sailing Yacht. Donald Street.

Blue Water Cruising. Bob & Nancy Griffith.

Understanding Rigs, and Rigging. Richard Henderson.

Sea Sense. Richard Henderson.

Cruising Routes. Jimmy Cornell.

Voyaging under Power. Beebe & Lieshman.

The Merck Manual. (Medical).

Heavy Weather Sailing. Adlard Coles.

50 Things You Must Know Before You Travel to Mexico. James Truette

http://tinyurl.com/29ths8

Cruising as a Way Of Life. Thomas Colvin.

The Boat Repair Manual. Buchanon.

Metal Boats. Bruce Roberts-Goodson.

Steel Away – A Guidebook to the World of Steel Sailboats. Smith & Moir

http://www.windroseaway.com/steelaway.html

Steel Boatbuilding : From Plans to Launching. Thomas Colvin.

Boatbuilding with Steel, Gilbert C. Klingel.

Boatbuilding with Aluminum, Stephen F. Pollard.

Cambium Woodworking Web Site.
http://www.cambiumbooks.com/books/boat_building/

Understanding Yacht Design. Ted Brewer

Sailing Yacht Designs. Bob Perry

The Desirable, and Undesirable Characteristics of Offshore Yachts. John Rousmaniere.

Lonely Planet, series of travel books. Go to the travel guides section.

http://www.lonelyplanet.com/

Safety Recommendations for Cruising Sailboats. [lx]

Practical Sailor – Tips, Tools & Techniques

http://www.practicalsailor.com/tools/features.html

Liveaboard Magazine
http://www.livingaboard.com/
or
http://tinyurl.com/2tp7lp

Knots, and Splices (ISBN: 0713634642)Cyrus Lawrence Day, et al.

ISF Publication "Pirates and Armed Robbers – A Masters' Guide"

Drug Trafficking and Abuse for Owners and Masters.

ICS & OCMIF. PERIL AT SEA AND SALVAGE: A GUIDE FOR MASTERS, 5TH ED., 1998

Smuggling in the Old Days

Smuggling in Cornwall
http://www.connexions.co.uk/culture/smuggler.htm

Smuggling & Shipwrecks
http://www.bl.uk/learning/langlit/texts/ship/shipwrecksandsmuggling.html

King's Cutters – the Revenue Service, and the War Against Smuggling

Outlaws of the Lakes: Bootlegging & Smuggling from Colonial Times to Prohibition

Sea Wolves, and Bandits

Tales of the Cornish Smugglers

The Scottish Smuggler

The Pirates Lafitte

Night Landing: A Short History of West Coast Smuggling : Heron, David ·

The Pirate Hunter, The True Story of Captain Kidd, By Richard Zacks

A sample of a rare book advertisement[119] for:

SMUGGLING IN CORNWALL BY FRANK GRAHAM

A Son of Australia. Memories of W.E. Parry-Okeden, ISO, 1840–1926

Brisbane, Watson, Ferguson, 1928. Octavo, xiv, 342 pages plus 19 plates. Gilt-decorated cloth; top edge lightly foxed; endpapers offset; essentially a very fine copy. At fourteen, Parry-Okeden was 'one of a Volunteer Force formed to assist in dealing with the trouble which culminated in the Ballarat riots'; after ten years of pastoral experience in Queensland, in 1870 he 'accepted the task of, organizing, training, and leading' the Border Patrol, formed to put an end to smuggling along the southern, and south-western borders of that colony; from 1895 to 1905, he was Commissioner of Police in Queensland. **$350**

119

http://www.treloars.com/catalogues/r99.htm

INDEX

2

20 Meters · 15, 56, 57, 58, 63

A

Accident · 2, 30, 31, 61
Admiralty Law · 95, 97, 173
Agent · 6, 19, 31, 104, 152
Aid · 3, 35
Aircraft · 26, 30, 37, 40, 97, 148, 149
Alameda · 30, 34
Amateur · 21, 62
Anchor · 38, 39, 81, 96, 98, 101, 153
Anchoring · 38, 39, 97, 98, 148
Archipelagic · 39, 97, 148
Arrested · 1, 2, 19, 23, 31, 36, 151, 152
Atlantic · 40, 69, 91
Attorney · 27, 94
Australia · 13, 14, 17, 18, 36, 39, 40, 41, 42, 89, 92, 153, 166
Authorities · 2
Automatic Identification System
    AIS · 53, 76, 98

B

Beacon · 36, 37, 59

Boat · i, xiii, xiv, xvi, xvii, xx, 1, 2, 7, 8, 9, 11, 14, 15, 16, 19, 20, 21, 23, 24, 25, 27, 28, 33, 44, 47, 52, 53, 54, 58, 61, 62, 78, 79, 80, 81, 82, 90, 94, 100, 101, 110, 111, 112, 116, 117, 124, 125, 128, 129, 130, 131, 132, 133, 160, 164, 165
Bootleg · xvii
Boundary · xvii, 61, 63, 96, 113, 156
Bridge-to-Bridge · xvii, 16, 56, 57, 58, 60, 63
Buoy · 68, 70, 73, 74

C

Call · 6, 9, 23, 27, 30, 31, 34, 38, 58, 83, 148, 151, 161, 162, 163, 164
Call Sign · 9
Canada · 3, 7, 8, 13, 21, 25, 26, 40, 69, 85, 89, 93, 135, 153
Canal · 84, 91, 164
Captain · i, xiv, xvi, 1, 2, 5, 8, 14, 15, 38, 81, 94, 95, 163, 164, 166
Carnet · 43, 44, 98
Centers for Disease Control
    CDC · 65, 66
Certificate · 44
CFR · 56, 57, 59, 60, 62, 63, 72, 78, 88, 93, 99, 101, 102
Citizen · xv, xvii, 34, 35, 42, 53

Clearance · xv, xvi, 4, 5, 6, 8, 9, 11, 14, 25, 26, 30, 33, 39, 63, 79, 95, 101, 102, 104
Clearance Number · 5, 6, 30, 101
Clearing · 1, 5, 8, 10, 13, 16, 25, 53, 79, 88
Coast Pilot · 17, 50, 51, 54, 55, 61, 62, 63, 71, 72
COLREG · xvii, 2, 60, 96
Compulsory · 51, 52, 54, 57, 58
Copy · 25, 46, 98
Corrections · xix
Credit · 27
Credit Card · 27
Crew · xiv, xvi, 1, 2, 19, 20, 38, 44, 51, 75, 152
Crime · 151, 152
Cruising · i, xv, xvi, 10, 11, 12, 13, 16, 20, 21, 27, 33, 45, 53, 62, 88, 91, 105, 165
Cruising Licenses · 11, 12, 62
Cuba · 28, 35, 60, 62, 89, 99, 153
Currency · 27, 88, 149
Customs
    Duty · 4, 8, 9, 11, 15, 34, 44, 53, 80, 88, 100, 157, 158, 159, 160, 161

D

Delaware · 12, 114, 128
Dialing · 83, 84, 85
Dinghy · 4, 9, 77, 78, 101
Direction · 73
Disease · 18, 64, 66, 67, 98
District · 11, 12, 51, 112, 114, 137, 138, 147
Documentation · 20, 27, 33, 49, 61, 75, 76, 77, 79, 80, 86, 87, 102

E

Early · 76
Embassy · xvii, 34, 36, 105, 106, 107
Emergency · 22, 23, 30, 34, 83, 85, 152, 161, 165, 172
Exempt · 2, 9, 11, 51, 54, 55, 61, 63, 110
Exemption · 14, 28, 44, 51, 58, 128
Expiration · 12, 20, 32, 41, 42, 86
Export · 28, 95, 99

F

FCC · 9, 16, 22, 32, 56, 57, 58, 59, 89, 100
Flag · 2, 26, 38, 46, 50, 51, 53, 63, 99
Florida · 6, 10, 12, 45, 48, 49, 113, 114, 128, 136, 137, 164
Foreign · i, xv, xvi, 1, 2, 3, 4, 5, 8, 11, 12, 14, 15, 20, 21, 23, 25, 26, 27, 35, 38, 46, 47, 50, 51, 53, 54, 57, 60, 63, 78, 79, 80, 88, 89, 91, 96, 97, 99, 100, 102, 106, 148, 150, 151, 152

G

Garbage · 9, 10, 32, 60
Government · 36, 41, 54, 92, 96
Guns · 10, 23

H

HAM · 21, 56, 59
High Seas · xvi, 1, 2, 21, 37, 79

Horn · 161

I

IALA · 68, 69, 73
Immigration · 8, 20, 97, 149
    Visa · 7, 8, 14, 41, 42
Import · 43
Inland · xvii, xviii, 3, 60, 91,
    118
Innocent · 38, 40, 57, 96, 97,
    148, 149, 150, 151
International Waters · 31, 37
Internet · xv, xviii, 48, 89, 90,
    111

J

Jail · i, xv, 1, 25, 29, 173

K

Knots · xiii, 81, 166

L

Lanes · 40, 71, 72, 150
License · 9, 10, 11, 12, 13, 16,
    21, 22, 23, 27, 28, 32, 53, 56,
    57, 58, 59, 62, 75, 88, 89, 99
Lights · 32, 73, 161, 162, 163
Logbook · 11, 32, 75, 93, 101
Lookout · 76, 161, 163

M

Marina · 110, 111
Master · xxi, 1, 46, 75, 100
Medical · xvii, 8, 19, 20, 64,
    75, 165

Mexico · 2, 13, 22, 23, 25, 26,
    44, 81, 82, 102, 116, 155,
    158, 165
MMSI · 9, 57, 100
Motor Vessel · 15

N

Night · 5, 29, 31, 33, 65, 67,
    70, 74, 109, 162, 163
Night Vision · 29, 67, 109, 163
Notes
    End Notes · xv, xviii, 89,
        172, 174
Notice · 3, 7, 16, 17, 18, 22, 32,
    66, 74, 75, 92, 93
Number · xv, xvi, xviii, 3, 5, 6,
    9, 10, 16, 17, 18, 25, 27, 30,
    31, 33, 45, 46, 47, 48, 49, 53,
    57, 59, 61, 68, 76, 77, 78, 82,
    83, 84, 86, 94, 100, 102, 114,
    119, 123

O

Officer · 23
Offshore · 30, 60, 113, 164,
    165
Operator · 32, 56, 57, 58, 59

P

Pacific · 85, 160
Passport · 41, 42, 98
Permit · 23, 28, 62, 123
Phone · 7, 45, 114, 122
Pilot · xiv, 32, 50, 51, 53, 54,
    55, 61, 63, 88, 104
Pilotage · 50, 51, 52, 53, 54
Piracy · xvi, 1, 35, 38, 90
Pirate · 81, 164, 166
Plot · 161

Portsmouth · 30, 34
Principle · 46, 101
Principle Use · 46, 101
Proof of Duty Paid · 25

R

Radio · xvii, 9, 21, 60, 62, 63,
  75
Reciprocal · 12
Reciprocity · 12, 45, 46, 88,
  101, 113, 122
Registration · xvi, 25, 37, 46,
  47, 49, 57, 79, 100, 113, 114,
  122
Regulation · 71
Renewal · 41, 76
Rescue · 30, 34, 36, 37, 164
Rights · ii, 38, 52

S

Sailing Directions · 3, 17, 33,
  71
Sales Tax · 47, 112, 123, 124,
  129, 131
Salvage · xv, 31, 172, 173
Single Side Band
  SSB · 22, 56, 58, 84
Smuggling · i, xvii, 1, 91, 166
Sojourners · 49
Stamp · 27, 96
Strait · 40, 51, 52, 55, 72, 148,
  154

T

Tax · xvi, xviii, 46, 47, 48, 75,
  102, 110, 111, 112, 113, 114,
  124, 125, 128, 129, 130, 131,
  133
Telephone · 83

Territorial · 13, 16, 31, 37, 96,
  97, 148, 149, 150, 151, 152,
  153, 154, 155
Title · 9, 10, 25, 45, 46, 47, 49,
  56, 59, 60, 61, 62, 63, 72, 88,
  101, 102, 103
Trade · 14, 38, 51, 52, 95, 174
Transient · 110
Transit · 40, 44

U

U.S. Code
  USC · 14, 57, 59, 93, 102
U.S. Customs · xxi, 5, 6, 7, 10,
  11, 12, 14, 25, 26, 29, 60, 62,
  90, 101, 134, 138
URL · xv, xviii, xix, 6, 18, 29,
  59, 60, 83, 89, 173
US Coast Guard · 50, 54, 61,
  80, 92, 93, 102
Use Tax · 46, 47, 49, 123

V

VAT · 102, 157, 158, 159, 160
Vessel · 1, 14, 15, 20, 26, 37,
  43, 44, 49, 58, 60, 61, 71, 77,
  80, 86, 87, 92, 99, 100, 101,
  102, 164
Vessel Traffic System · xvii,
  58, 71, 72
VHF · 22, 31, 56, 58, 76, 98,
  162

W

Waiver · 7
Washington · 6, 7, 12, 34, 51,
  52, 83, 108, 110, 113, 118,
  127, 134, 138, 164
Watch · 11, 58, 161

Web · xvii, xix, 7, 9, 18, 49,
62, 65, 67, 89, 92, 105, 126,
165

Web Site · xvii, 9, 18, 62, 67,
89, 105, 165

Forthcoming Books from Capt. Mike

 See author's web site:

http://www.yachtsdelivered.com/bookpub.html

Salvage - [120]

 Remember that you have a copy of the salvage form, here at the very back of the book, in your *Emergency Kit,* just past the End Notes, on page 174. Better to rip up this book than to be without a Salvage Form, if you need one!

U.S. Coast Guard Emergency Numbers, see page 34.

BoatUS Salvage

http://tinyurl.com/36sygn [lxi]

PDF version

http://tinyurl.com/2kkdsq [lxii]

---

[120] *I require assistance*

Salvage has a defined meaning.

There must be service which deserves a reward.

There must be danger.

The service must be voluntary.

Success is required. An effort to save a vessel from sinking that fails, does not create a salvage award.

Salvage of lives is required of the master of any vessel in a position to do so, on penalty of fines and jail time. A dead body is not a life and is subject to salvage.

A vessel which is abandoned, a derelict, is subject to salvage. When the owner returns the salvage must cease if requested. Salvage awards in such a case depends upon the service rendered.

Ordinary towing is not salvage.[121]

A salvage contract can be verbal, but a written one should be implemented as soon as practical.

Salvage awards are settled in Admiralty Court, if not agreed to outside of court.

The salvage form included with this book provides for local arbitration, under the principles of Admiralty Law.

See this URL for a clearly written description by a maritime lawyer. *Understanding The Difference Between Towing & Salvage* by Stephen White.

http://www.offshorerisk.com/definitions/salvage.htm

---

[121] Emanuel Stavroudis, 23 F. (2d) 214

End Notes

Each End Note is associated with a *tinyurl.com* link, back in the main text. The End Notes use the Roman (i, v) numerals as distinct from the Latin (1, 5) numerals used to denote Footnotes.

---

[i] http://www.yachtsdelivered.com/bookpub.html

[ii] http://ask.yahoo.com/20030103.html

[iii] http://www.tc.gc.ca/acts-regulations/GENERAL/C/CSA/regulations/010/csa014/csa14.html

[iv] http://www.cbp.gov/xp/cgov/travel/pleasure_boats/boats/pleasure_locations/

[v] http://www.cbp.gov/xp/cgov/travel/pleasure_boats/boats/oars.xml

[vi] http://www.cbp.gov/xp/cgov/toolbox/publications/trade/

[vii] http://www.cbp.gov/xp/cgov/travel/vaction/ready_set_go/sea_travel/material/

[viii] http://www.cbp.gov/xp/cgov/travel/vacation/kbyg/

[ix] http://www.cbp.gov/linkhandler/cgov/toolbox/legal/directives/3130-006.ctt/3130-006.txt

[x] http://www.the-triton.com/megayachtnews/index.php?news=827

[xi] http://www.customs.gov.au/site/page.cfm?u=4791

xii http://www.wcoomd.org/tariff/?v=3

xiii http://www.arrl.org/FandES/field/regulations/io/#iarpcountries

xiv
http://www.erodocdb.dk/docs/implement_doc_adm.aspx?docid=
1802

xv http://en.wikipedia.org/wiki/Citizens'_band_radio

xvi
http://www.cbp.gov/xp/cgov/travel/pleasure_boats/user_fee/user_
fee_decal.xml

xvii http://www.cbp.gov/xp/cgov/toolbox/forms/

xviii http://en.wikipedia.org/wiki/Power_of_attorney

xix http://www.pmddtc.state.gov/country.htm

xx http://www.bis.doc.gov/licensing/exportingbasics.htm

xxi http://www.state.gov/countries

xxii
http://travel.state.gov/travel/tips/emergencies/emergencies_1199.
html

xxiii http://www.geosalliance.com/index.html

xxiv https://beaconregistration.noaa.gov/rgdb/

xxv
http://beacons.amsa.gov.au/Buying_and_registering/Registration.a
sp#top

xxvi http://www.mcga.gov.uk/c4mca/mcga-hmcg_rescue/mcga-
hmcg-sar/epirb.htm

xxvii http://en.wikipedia.org/wiki/Strait

xxviii http://en.wikipedia.org/wiki/Visa_Waiver_Program

xxix http://en.wikipedia.org/wiki/Electronic_Travel_Authority

xxx http://onlinestore.cch.com/default.asp?bu=fast&view=expand

xxxi
http://books.google.com/books?id=gMqgJzEhFNcC&pg=PA112
7&lpg=PA1127&dq=%22sales+tax%22+%22use+tax%22+boats

&source=web&ots=OaaJ2fCXdY&sig=yx5XKtDsWKQxL123lC
CG-jxxTO8#PPA9,M1

xxxii http://www.marinetitle.com/index.htm

xxxiii http://www.boatus.com/gov/state_boat.asp

xxxiv http://www.dmv.org/boatregistration.php

xxxv http://www.boatus.com/gov/state_doc.asp

xxxvi http://www.nasbla.org/references.php#Numbering

xxxvii http://www.uscgboating.org/regulations/boating_laws.htm

xxxviii http://dor.mflorida.com/dor/taxes/sut_boat_owner.html

xxxix http://frwebgate.access.gpo.gov/cgi-bin/get-
cfr.cgi?TITLE=47&PART=80&SECTION=1&TYPE=TEXT
xl

http://www.ustreas.gov/offices/enforcement/ofac/programs/cuba/cuba.s
html
xli

http://www.ustreas.gov/offices/enforcement/ofac/programs/ascii/cuba.t
xt

xlii http://www.uscg.mil/d7/d7o/mic/cubapermit.htm
xliii

http://www.gulfcoastmariners.org/research%20reports/HTML/R-
223/R-223r2.htm

xliv http://hyperphysics.phy-astr.gsu.edu/hbase/vision/rodcone.html

xlv http://health.howstuffworks.com/question53.htm

xlvi http://en.wikipedia.org/wiki/Rod_cell

xlvii http://www.visualexpert.com/Resources/nightvision.html

xlviii http://en.wikipedia.org/wiki/Sea_mark

xlix http://www.deck-officer.info/buoyage/ialamap.jpg

l http://www.cgate.co.il/eng/Seamanship/buoy_lateral.htm

li http://en.wikipedia.org/wiki/Cardinal_mark

[lii] http://www.uscg.mil/hq/gm/vdoc/forms/cg1280.pdf

[liii] http://www.uscg.mil/hq/gm/vdoc/genpub.htm

[liv] http://www.access.gpo.gov/nara/cfr/waisidx_07/46cfr67_07.html

[lv] http://en.wikipedia.org/wiki/List_of_country_calling_codes

[lvi] http://www.amazon.co.uk/RYA-European-Waterways-Regulations-Explained/dp/0954730100

[lvii] http://www.nga.mil/portal/site/maritime/?epi_menuItemID=2fbece2b0f5de897dc3f8c107d27a759&epi_menuID=e106a3b5e50edce1fec24fd73927a759&epi_baseMenuID=e106a3b5e50edce1fec24fd73927a759

[lviii] http://www.uscg.mil/hq/gm/vdoc/nvdc.htm

[lix] http://www.plymouth.gov.uk/homepage/leisureandtourism/libraries/whatsinyourlibrary/lns/navalsayings/navalsayingsac.htm

[lx] http://www.ussailing.org/merchandise/detail.asp?product_id=51025

[lxi] http://www.boatus.com/towing/guide/salvage/contract.asp

[lxii] http://www.boatus.com/salvage/contract.pdf

Left Blank

STANDARD FORM YACHT SALVAGE CONTRACT

Boat Owners Association of The United States

STANDARD FORM YACHT SALVAGE CONTRACT

It is hereby agreed this _____ day of _____, 20___,

at _____ hours at _____ (location)

by and between:_____ (Owner or Captain)

for the Yacht named "_____,"

which is described as a ("Vessel") _____

(yr - manufacturer - length)

and insured by: _____ ("Underwriter")

and _____, (Salvage

Company/Salvor)

to salvage the yacht under these terms and conditions:

1. Salvor agrees to render assistance to and endeavor to save said yacht and its property and deliver her afloat or ashore at _____ marina or port as mutually agreed, or to nearest safe port if unspecified herein, as soon as practicable.

2. Salvor shall have the requisite possession and control of the subject yacht and be entitled without expense to the reasonable use of the yacht and its gear in the performance of recovery or salvage operations.

3. Said salvage and any towage services by the Salvor shall terminate upon delivery of said yacht as designated herein. Owner and Underwriter shall be responsible for any storage, towing or other port or marina charges following delivery and for risk of loss thereafter.

(a) NO CURE/NO PAY (Compensation, including special compensation, to be determined under ARTICLES 13 and 14, SALCON 89, and U.S. Admiralty Law.)

INITIALS _____/_____ salvor/owner

(b) NO CURE/NO PAY, AT A FIXED PRICE of $_____

INITIALS _____/_____ salvor owner

(c) NO CURE/NO PAY at $_____/per hour/per day/per vessel (or in accordance with SALVOR's published rates, initialed and attached hereto).

INITIALS _____/_____ salvor /owner

(d) OTHER: _____

STANDARD FORM YACHT SALVAGE CONTRACT

Compensation to Salvor for the services performed hereunder shall be in accordance with a billing and any supportive analysis of the salvage operation to be presented to Owner and underwriter's agents upon completion of salvage. Billing to be calculated on the basis specified in No. 3. No agreement on price or its reasonableness has been made at the scene unless agreed to in writing.

5. Services hereunder are rendered on a "No Cure, No Pay" basis; however, salvor shall be entitled to a reasonable allowance for prevention or minimization of environmental damage in accordance with Articles 13 & 14 of the 1989 International Convention on Salvage, as well as for clean up or wreck removal in the event the vessel is deemed a constructive total loss. Payment is due promptly upon presentation of Salvor's bill. Interest at the rate of one and one-half (1.5%) percent per month (or the maximum legal rate allowed) shall accrue on any unpaid balance from 30 days after completion of salvage and presentation if a salvage bill, or as determined in accordance with the findings of any Arbitration Award.

6. In the event of any dispute regarding this salvage or concerning the reasonableness of any fees or charges due hereunder, all parties agree to binding local arbitration utilizing individual(s) experienced in maritime and salvage law. The Boat Owners Association of The United States Salvage Arbitration Plan, though not required, is available as a public service through Boat Owners Association of The United States wherever the parties agree to its use. In the event Owner is uninsured for payment of these services, Salvor may, at its election, agree with Owner to use any agreeable arbitration system or to proceed with all available legal remedies to recover sums believed due and owing.

7. It is understood that services performed hereunder are governed by the Admiralty and Maritime Jurisdiction of the Federal Courts and create a maritime lien against the yacht or its posted security. Salvor's lien shall be preserved until payment. Salvor agrees in lieu of arrest or attachment to accept from the yacht's Underwriter, a Letter of Undertaking for an amount equal to one and one-half (1.5) times the presented billing with a copy of the insurance policy and coverage information. If the yacht is uninsured or its Underwriter cannot provide a Letter of Undertaking, Salvor may demand the posting of a Surety Bond with its designated Escrow Agent in an amount equal to 1.5 times the Salvor's bill. Salvor may satisfy collection of fees or charges hereunder by recourse to any security posted and shall be entitled to any costs incurred in collection of payments due hereunder including reasonable attorneys fees subject to the findings of any arbitration.

8. Salvor hereby warrants that it is acting on its own behalf and on behalf of any subcontractors retained by Salvor to perform services in the recovery or delivery of the yacht. Salvor shall be responsible for any such subcontractors' compensation.

9. In the event the Salvor has already rendered salvage services to the described yacht prior to execution of this contract, the provisions of this contract shall apply to such salvage services.

STANDARD FORM YACHT SALVAGE CONTRACT

SIGNED:_____
  Owner/Captain or Owner's Agent

SIGNED:_____
  Salvage Company

  Owner Print Name & Address: _____

_____

_____

Phone: (____) _____ Fax: (____) _____

  Salvor Print Name & Address: _____

_____

_____

Phone: (____) _____Fax: (____) _____